SPRING AWAKENING

A CHILDREN'S TRAGEDY

BY
FRANK WEDEKIND

TRANSLATED BY
JONATHAN FRANZEN

★

DRAMATISTS
PLAY SERVICE
INC.

SPRING AWAKENING
Copyright © 2008, Jonathan Franzen

All Rights Reserved

SPECIAL NOTE

SPRING AWAKENING
by Frank Wedekind
Translated by Jonathan Franzen

The translator is grateful to Benjamin Moser for his careful reading of the text and his many valuable suggestions.

AUTHENTIC BUT HORRIBLE:
AN INTRODUCTION TO *SPRING AWAKENING*

Frank Wedekind was a lifelong guitar player. If he'd been born a hundred years later, he almost certainly would have been a rock star; the only small reason to doubt it is that he grew up in Switzerland. Whether you consider it a boon or a sorrow that he instead became the author of *Spring Awakening*, the best and most enduring German play of its era, depends a lot on what you value in a work of art. The great strengths of *Spring Awakening* — comedy, character, language — are mostly incidental to good rock. But the play, while lacking in mass appeal, also manages to partake of some of rock's own strengths: its youthful energy, its disruptive power, its feeling of *authenticity*. Indeed, decades after the shocks of Elvis and Jimi Hendrix and the Sex Pistols have ceased to shock anyone, *Spring Awakening* has become, if anything, even more of a disturbance and a reproach than it was a century ago. What the playwright sacrificed in amplification he's making up for in longevity.

Conceived in California and christened Benjamin Franklin, Wedekind was the son of an itinerant young singer/actress and a politically radical physician twice her age. His mother had left Europe at the age of sixteen to follow her sister and brother-in-law to Valparaiso, Chile. The brother-in-law soon ran into financial trouble, which the two sisters alleviated by touring as singers along the coasts of South and Central America, and when the sister died of yellow fever, Frank's mother moved to San Francisco and supported her brother-in-law's family by working as a performer. She was twenty-two when she married Dr. Friedrich Wedekind, who had emigrated from Germany soon after the suppressed political revolts of 1848. Returning to Germany, where Frank was born in 1864, Dr. Wedekind gave up his medical practice and devoted himself to full-time political agitation. The country's mood was becoming increasingly hostile and Bismarckian, however, and by 1872 the family had settled permanently in a small castle in Switzerland.

Though the Wedekind marriage was a stormy one, the family was big and close-knit and intellectually sophisticated. Frank was well liked both at home and at school. By the time he finished high school, he was writing plays and poetry as well as songs that he sang to the accompaniment of his guitar. He'd become a radical atheist and was at once ruggedly well-adjusted and profoundly unfit for conventional employment and a middle-class life. He and his father argued so violently about his career that he finally assaulted the old man and left for Munich to become a professional writer. He wrote *Spring Awakening* in the winter of 1890–91, finishing it on Easter Day. For the next fifteen years he worked to ingratiate himself with the theater world and get his plays produced. His good friends included a shady art dealer and a circus performer, Willy Rudinoff, who was renowned as a fire-eater and birdsong imitator. Wedekind once tried to get a circus to produce his work. He founded and performed in a Munich cabaret called the Eleven Executioners. Over the years, he took to the stage himself more and more, both to forge relationships with theaters and, increasingly, to showcase the anti-naturalistic rhythms with which he intended his later plays to be performed. In 1906, as success and fame were finally arriving, he married a very young actress, Tilly Newes, whom he had cultivated for the role of Lulu in his plays *Pandora's Box* and *Earth Spirit* (after the basis for the Alban Berg opera *Lulu*). The couple had two daughters, who would later remember their father treating children with exceptional respect, as if there were no significant difference between children and adults.

Due partly to the rigors of acting, Wedekind sickened during the years of the First World War and died, in 1918, from complications of abdominal surgery. At his funeral, in Munich, there was a riot worthy of a rock star. Many of Germany's leading literary lights, including the young Bertolt Brecht, were at the cemetery, but so was a mob of the young and the strange and the crazy — members of a cultural and sexual bohemia that had recognized in Wedekind a freak with the courage of his freakdom — and these mourners stormed across the graveyard, rushing for good places beside the open grave. An unstable poet named Heinrich Lautensack, one of the other Eleven Executioners, threw a wreath of roses on the coffin and then jumped down into the grave, crying, "To Frank Wedekind, my teacher, my model, my master, from your least worthy pupil!" while a friend of Lautensack's, a moviemaker from Berlin, filmed the whole thing for posterity. The exhibitionist mourner and his complicit cameraman: a rock-and-roll world was already in sight.

One useful example of the ongoing danger and vitality of *Spring Awakening* was the insipid rock-musical version of it that opened on Broadway in 2006, a hundred years after the play's world premiere, and was instantly overpraised. The script that Wedekind had finished in 1891 was far too frank sexually to be producible on any late-Victorian stage. When the play finally did begin to appear in theaters, fifteen years later, no local government in Germany or abroad would let it go uncut. And yet even the cruelest bowdlerizations of a century ago were milder than the maiming a dangerous play now undergoes in becoming a contemporary hit.

The hand-wringing young Moritz Stiefel, whom Wedekind had kill himself over a bad report card, is transformed, in the musical version, into a punk rocker of such talent and charisma that it's unimaginable that a report card could depress him. The casual rape of Wendla Bergmann by the play's central character, Melchior Gabor, becomes a thunderous spectacle of ecstasy and consent. And where Wedekind showed the young sensualist Hansy Rilow *resisting* masturbation — reluctantly destroying a piece of pornography that threatens to "eat away" his brain — we in the twenty-first century are treated to a choreographed orgy of penis-pumping, semen-slinging exultation. Wedekind, without resorting to anything more obscene than a few comically high-flown double entendres, got Hansy's plight exactly right. He knew that the real fuel of the masturbator's shame is solitude, he nailed the masturbator's weirdly personal tenderness for the virtual object, he understood the corrosive autonomy of sexual images; but this would all be uncomfortably pertinent to our porn-soaked modernity, and so the musical is obliged to sanitize Wedekind and render Hansy's torments as something merely dirty. (The result is "funny" in the same way that bad sitcoms are "funny": viewers emit nervous laughter at every mention of sex and then, hearing themselves laugh, conclude that what they're watching must be hilarious.) As for the working-class girl Martha Bessel, who in the original play is beaten by her father and ardently envied for these beatings by the bourgeois masochist Wendla Bergmann: What else could she become in 2006 but a saintly young emblem of *sexual* abuse? Her supportive, sisterly friends join her in singing "The Dark I Know Well," an anthem to the sorrow of being carnally interesting to grown-ups. Instead of Martha's appalling matter-of-factness about her home life (she says she's beaten "only if there's something special"), there is now a dense modern fog of sentimentality and bad faith. A team of grown-ups creates a musical whose main selling point is teen sex (the first Broadway posters showed the male lead mounting the female lead) and whose female teen characters, shortly after wailing to their largely grown-up audience that they are bad-girl love-junkies, come forward to sing of how terribly, unfairly painful it is to possess a teen sexuality that fascinates grownups. If the path from Bratz dolls through Britneywear finally leaves a girl feeling like somebody else's piece of meat, it obviously can't be commercial culture's fault, because commercial culture has such a rockin' great sound track and nobody understands teenagers better than commercial culture does, nobody admires them more than it does, nobody works harder to make them feel authentic, nobody insists more strenuously that young consumers are *always right,* whether as moral heroes or as moral victims. So something else must be to blame: maybe the amorphous tyranny that rock and roll still imagines itself to be rebelling against, maybe those nameless tyrants who make the stultifying rules that commercial culture is forever urging us to break. Maybe them. In the end, the only thing that really matters to teenagers is that they be taken very seriously. And here, among all the ways in which *Spring Awakening* would seem to be unsuitable material for a commercial rock musical, is Frank Wedekind's most grievous offense: He makes fun of teenagers — flat-out laughs at them — to the same degree that he takes them seriously. And so now, more than ever, he must be censored.

The term Wedekind chose as a subtitle for his play, *A Children's Tragedy,* has an odd, unresolvable, almost comic ring to it. It sounds as if tragedy were stooping to get through the door of a playhouse, or as if kids were tripping on the hems of grown-up costumes. Although the eleven o'clock news may use the word "tragedy" when an adolescent commits suicide, the conventional attributes of a tragic figure — power, importance, self-destructive hubris, a capacity for mature moral self-reckoning — are by definition beyond the reach of children. And what are we to make of a "tragedy" in which the central character, Melchior Gabor, survives intact?

Over the years, many critics and producers have come to terms with Wedekind's subtitle by reading the play as a kind of revolutionary systems tragedy. In these readings, the position of tragic hero is occupied not by an individual but by an entire society which is destroying the children it claims to love. The earliest German productions of *Spring Awakening* highlighted those aspects of the play suggesting that Wendla and Moritz and Melchior are springlike vital innocents who fall victim to a nineteenth-century bourgeois morality that has outlived itself. For Emma Goldman, writing in 1914, the play was "a powerful indictment" of the "misery and torture" of children growing up in "sex ignorance." For the English playwright and director Edward Bond, writing sixty years later, the play functioned as a denunciation of a "technological society" in which "everything depends on conformity to routine." The problem with these interpretations is not that they're factually untenable — the play does, after all, produce a couple of wrenching deaths — but that they undervalue the play's line-by-line humor. As early as 1911, Wedekind was defending his text against overly earnest political readings, insisting that he'd intended the play to be a "sunny image of life" in which, in all but one of the scenes, he had tried to exploit a "freewheeling humor" for all the laughs that he could get.

The critic and playwright Eric Bentley, the author of the least incomplete English translation of *Spring Awakening* to date, grants Wedekind's point about the laughs but offers the incriminating subtitle as evidence that the playwright was protesting too much. Leaving aside the possibility that the subtitle might simply be ironic, or that it's echoing Goethe's *Faust*, which is also hardly the tragedy that its subtitle promises, Bentley proposes that *Spring Awakening* be read as a "tragicomedy." However sunny or unsunny an image of life it may present, the play is undeniably saturated, from the very first page, with premonitions of death and violence. And the word "tragicomedy" does, in its very awkwardness, like "children's tragedy," feel true to the doomy absurdities of young love: the laughability of adolescent sorrows, the sorrows of adolescent laughability.

What the word feels less true to is the actual action of the play. Dramatic tragedy, whether Greek or Shakespearean or modern or even half comic, makes sense only in the context of a morally ordered universe. *(This is what happens to otherwise excellent people, Mr. Hamlet, when they get too self-conscious. This is what happens, Mr. Loman, when you take the big lie of the American Dream home from work with you.)* Tragedy always pays off with the affirmation of some kind of cosmic justice, however cruel, which the audience recognizes from its experience of life. And what's really shocking about *Spring Awakening* — what was shocking in 1906 and, to judge from the vigor of the Broadway musical's suppression of it, no less shocking in 2006 — is how casually and thoroughly amoral the play's action is. That both Wendla Bergmann and Moritz Stiefel are initially preoccupied with death may make their later fates seem inevitable; but tragedy requires more than just inevitability. In what morally comprehensible universe does a goofy, vivid, lovable character like Moritz

Stiefel *necessarily* meet an untimely end? His death, like so many teen suicides, is random, contingent, meaningless — and thus fully in keeping with the worldview of his atheist friend Melchior, who, by his own account, believes in "nothing in the world at all." The grown-ups in charge of the play's action are no less helpless than Moritz. You can hate Headmaster Hart-Payne and the other school administrators for their authoritarianism, but they are facing a "suicide epidemic" that they're completely unequipped to make sense of. Their crime is being grown-up and stuffy and unimaginative; they're insecure buffoons, not morally culpable killers. Similarly, you can hate Mr. Gabor for his coldhearted condemnation of his son, but the fact remains that his son sexually assaulted a girl he didn't love, just for the sensation of it, and can't be trusted not to do it again.

The only intelligible ways to judge the characters in *Spring Awakening* are comic and aesthetic, not moral. And so we're thrown back on Wedekind's insistence that his children's tragedy is, in fact, a comedy. Moritz, on the verge of blowing his brains out, resolves to think of whipped cream when he pulls the trigger. ("It's filling and it leaves behind a pleasant aftertaste.") Ilse tells Martha that she knows why Moritz shot himself ("Parallelepiped!") and refuses to give Martha the suicide gun ("I'm saving it as a souvenir"). Wendla, confined to bed by her swelling belly ("our terrible indigestion," in the doctor's words), declares that she is dying of dropsy. "You don't have dropsy," her mother replies, "you have a *baby*." At which point Wedekind, following through on a wonderful joke that he set up ten scenes earlier, when Mrs. Bergmann told Wendla that babies come from marriage, delivers the double punch line:

WENDLA. But that's not possible, Mother. I'm not married…!
MRS. BERGMANN. Great God Almighty — that's just it, you're not married!

Mrs. Bergmann, who is herself so guileless that she lets Mr. Gabor take Melchior's legally incriminating letter away from her, is last seen telling Wendla sugary, protective lies as she ushers an abortionist neighbor into Wendla's sickroom. There are, to be sure, a few genuinely vile adult characters in the play — Moritz's father, Reverend Bleekhead, Dr. Procrustes — but some of the minor male adolescent characters are no less vile, and Wendla's friend Thea shows signs of becoming every bit as conformist and narrow-minded as her parents. The more important adult characters all reveal at least some shred of humanity, if only in the form of fear. Indeed, they not only *do* reveal it, they *must* reveal it; otherwise they couldn't be the subjects of real comedy. To laugh well at humanity, both your own humanity and that of others, you have to be as distant and unsparing as if you're writing tragedy. Unlike tragedy, though, comedy doesn't require a grand moral scheme. Comedy is the more rugged genre and the one better suited to godless times. Comedy requires only that you have a heart that can recognize other hearts. Although it's true that Mrs. Bergmann's timidity leads directly to the death of her beloved daughter, this human frailty is also what makes Mrs. Bergmann a full-blooded comic character, rather than just a stock satiric type. You'd have to be a morally absolutist teenager — or a contemporary pop-culture provider pandering to morally absolutist teenagers — not to feel compassion for Mrs. Bergmann in the world of trouble her fear has landed her in.

And just as the adult principals could not be unredeemably bad and still be funny, so the child principals could not be purely good. Moritz's self-pity and his obsession with suicide, Melchior's sadism and amorality, Wendla's masochism and almost vindictively willful ignorance, Hansy's cynical carnality: The cruelest blow that *Spring Awakening* delivers to contemporary pieties, the deep embarrassment that the Broadway musical seeks to camouflage with raunchier shames, is that Wedekind treats his child characters like fascinating little animals — flawed, adorable, dangerous, silly. They fall far to either side of the safe teen middle ground of coolness and righteousness. They're at once unbearably innocent and unbearably corrupt.

Toward the end of his life, Wedekind compiled a list of adjectives to describe himself in contrast to his contemporary and rival dramatist Gerhardt Hauptmann. At the bottom of the list of Wedekind's own attributes were the words "authentic but horrible." The funniness and sadness and resignation of this self-description are the spirit of *Spring Awakening*.

In translating *Spring Awakening*, I've made it my first priority to leave nothing out. This particularly includes the play's original punctuation, which was unusual even in the 1890s for its profusion of dashes. Wedekind uses the dashes to indicate broken-off speech, silences, and abrupt changes in tempo or tone. He also invariably places a dash after a punch line, thus making the dashes a reliable guide to his comic intentions. One could argue that Wedekind was trying to micromanage future actors, but actors are always free to disregard the punctuation, and readers, I think, will appreciate the instruction in the rhythms of the work, particularly the comic rhythms.

My effort to be complete extends also to the welter of tones in the original — Mrs. Bergmann's cloying baby talk, Hansy's arch lyricism, Moritz's maudlin mooning, Ilse's loopy depravity, Mrs. Gabor's self-adoring liberalism, and so forth. Otherwise insightful translations by Edward Bond and by the poet Ted Hughes have been diminished, in Bond's case, by a tendentious tone of *épater les bourgeois* and, in Hughes's case, by a penchant for blunt, short, declarative sentences. Even Eric Bentley takes shortcuts when confronted with deliriously tangled phrases of Hart-Payne's such as "*den Gymnasiasten an seine durch sein Heranbildung zum Gebildeten gebildeten Existenzbedingungen zu fesseln.*" (Literally: "to shackle the high-school student to the existential requirements that his education into a state of education entail.") One sympathizes with Bentley for reducing this to "to teach the boys the obligations of an educated existence," but his version is neither complete nor accurate nor, more damagingly, funny.

My other priority has been to render Wedekind's lines in such a way that an English-speaking actor has some hope of sounding natural while speaking them. After Moritz's suicide attempt has been interrupted by the surprise appearance of Ilse, he laments his bad luck by screaming, "*Dieses Glückskind, dieses Sonnenkind — dieses Freudenmädchen auf meinem Jammerweg!*" which Eric Bentley renders as "this child of fortune, child of sunshine, daughter of joy upon my way of sorrows!" This is not an easy English line to speak, let alone scream. It also crucially omits the dash between the second and third phrases, which is there to suggest a distraught Moritz catching himself in midutterance and correcting his own high-flown language with the more honest word "*Freudenmädchen*" — i.e., joy-girl, i.e., prostitute. "Daughter of joy," while technically accurate, is an archaic term with no comic punch. Edward Bond here offers "little whore," which is (typically for Bond) at once too strong and reasonably true to the dramatic moment. Ted Hughes stretches things with "blissful temptress," which is (typically for Hughes) both interesting and somehow not right. My own best shot is "floozy." Given the greatness and mystery of *Spring Awakening*, this is surely just the latest word, not the last.

—Jonathan Franzen

CHARACTERS

Children

Wendla Bergmann
Melchior Gabor
Moritz Stiefel
Ilse
Martha Bessel
Thea
Hansy Rilow
Ernst Röbel
George Zirschnitz
Robert
Otto Lämmermeier

Boys in the Reformatory

Diethelm
Reinhold
Rupert
Helmuth
Gaston

Adults

Mrs. Bergmann
Mrs. Gabor
Mr. Gabor
A Lawyer
Mr. Stiefel
A Pensioner
Ina Müller
Headmaster Hart-Payne
Professor Brockenbohn
Professor Starver
Professor Schmalz

Professor Blodgett
Professor Fitztongue
Professor Killaflye
Reverend Bleekhead
Ziegenmelker, a friend of Mr. Stiefel's
Uncle Probst
Fetch
Dr. Seltzer, the Public Health Officer
Dr. Procrustes
A Locksmith
The Masked Man

PLACE

The play is set in provincial Germany.

TIME

1892.

To the masked man
—*The Author*

SPRING AWAKENING

ACT ONE

Scene 1

A living room.

WENDLA. Why did you make me such a long dress, Mother?

MRS. BERGMANN. It's your fourteenth birthday!

WENDLA. If I'd known you'd make my dress so long, I wouldn't have wanted to be fourteen.

MRS. BERGMANN. This dress is not too long, Wendla. What do you want me to do? Can I help it if my baby is two inches taller every spring? Now that you're a grown-up girl, you can't expect to go out in a pinafore.

WENDLA. At least my pinafore looks better on me than this bathrobe. — Please let me keep wearing it! Just for the summer. This sackcloth is going to fit me the same whether I'm fourteen or fifteen. — Let's put it away till my next birthday; I'd only be stepping on the hem and tearing it.

MRS. BERGMANN. I don't know what to say to you. I'd love to keep you just the way you are, baby. Other girls your age are skinny and gawky. You're the opposite. — Who knows what you'll be like when the others are fully developed.

WENDLA. Who knows — maybe I won't be around anymore.

MRS. BERGMANN. Baby, baby, where do you get these ideas?

WENDLA. Don't, Mommy; don't be sad!

MRS. BERGMANN. *(Kissing her.)* My dearest darling!

WENDLA. I get them at night when I can't fall asleep. I don't feel sad at all, and I know I'll sleep all the better then. — Mother, is it sinful to think about things like that?

MRS. BERGMANN. Go and hang the sackcloth in the closet! Put your pinafore back on, for heaven's sake! — When I have a chance, I'll sew a ruffle on the bottom.

WENDLA. *(Hanging the dress in the closet.)* No, in that case I'd rather go ahead and be twenty…!

MRS. BERGMANN. Just as long as you don't get too cold! — That little dress used to be plenty long for you; but …

WENDLA. Now, when it's almost summer? — Oh, Mother, even children don't get diphtheria in the back of their knees! You're such a worrier. A person doesn't get cold at my age — your legs least of all. Would it be better if I got too hot, Mother? — You can thank the good Lord if your dearest darling doesn't cut her sleeves off one of these mornings and run into you some evening in the twilight without any shoes and socks on! — When I wear my sackcloth, I'm going to be dressed like a fairy queen underneath … Don't be angry, Mommy! No one will ever know it then.

Scene 2

Sunday evening.

MELCHIOR. This is too boring. I'm going to quit.

OTTO. Then the rest of us will have to stop too. — Have you done the homework, Melchior?

MELCHIOR. Just keep playing!

MORITZ. Where are you going?

MELCHIOR. For a walk.

GEORGE. It's getting awfully dark.

ROBERT. Have you done the homework already?

MELCHIOR. Why shouldn't I go for a walk in the dark?

ERNST. Central America! — Louis the Fifteenth! — Sixty lines of Homer! — Seven equations!

MELCHIOR. Damn this homework!

GEORGE. If only the Latin paper wasn't due tomorrow, too!

MORITZ. There's nothing you can think about without homework getting in the way!

OTTO. I'm going home.

GEORGE. Me too, I've got homework.

ERNST. Me too, me too.

ROBERT. Good night, Melchior.

MELCHIOR. Sleep well! *(All except Moritz and Melchior leave.)* What I'd like to know is what are we doing in this world, anyway?

MORITZ. As far as school is concerned, I'd rather be a cab horse! — What do we go to school for? — We go to school so they can give us exams! — And what do they give us exams for? — So we can flunk. — Seven of us have to flunk, if only because the upstairs classroom doesn't hold more than sixty. — I've felt so peculiar since Christmas … I swear to God, if it weren't for my dad I'd pack a bag tonight and go to Altona Harbor!

MELCHIOR. Let's talk about something else. — *(They go for a walk.)*

MORITZ. You see that black cat there with its tail in the air?

MELCHIOR. Do you believe in omens?

MORITZ. I'm not sure. — It came from over there. It doesn't mean anything.

MELCHIOR. This is a Charybdis that I think everyone falls into if they've managed to escape the Scylla of religious superstition. — Let's sit down here under the beech tree. There's a warm spring wind blowing over the mountains. I'd like to be a young dryad now and spend the whole long night up there in the woods, swinging and rocking in the highest treetops …

MORITZ. Unbutton your vest, Melchior!

MELCHIOR. Ha — the way it makes your clothes puff out!

MORITZ. God, it's getting so pitch-dark you can't even see your hand in front of your face. In fact, where are you? — Don't you agree, Melchior, that a human being's sense of shame is merely a product of his upbringing?

MELCHIOR. I was giving this some thought just the day before yesterday. No matter what, the feeling does seem to be deeply rooted in human nature. Imagine that you're supposed to take off all your clothes in front of your best friend. You wouldn't do it unless he was doing it himself at the same time. — I guess it's also more or less a fashion thing.

MORITZ. I've been thinking that when I have children, little boys and girls, I'm going to start them out sleeping in the same room, if possible in the very same bed, and have them help each other get dressed and undressed every morning and every night, and when the weather's hot both the girls and the boys are not going to wear anything all day except short white woolen tunics with leather belts. — It seems to me that, if they grow up like this, then later on they're bound to be more relaxed than we are, as a rule.

MELCHIOR. That's definitely my opinion, Moritz! — The only question is, what happens when the girls start having babies?

MORITZ. What do you mean, having babies?

MELCHIOR. Well, in this regard, I believe in certain instincts. I believe, for example, that if you take a male cat and a female cat and you shut them up together when they're still young, and you keep the two of them isolated from all contact with the outside world — that is, if you leave them entirely to their own inclinations — that sooner or later the female is going to get pregnant, even though neither she nor the male had anyone whose example they could follow.

MORITZ. I guess with animals it eventually just happens.

MELCHIOR. All the more so with people, is what I think! Listen, Moritz, if your boys are sleeping in the very same bed with the girls, and all of a sudden they feel their first masculine stirrings — I'll bet you anything ...

MORITZ. You may be right about that. — But still ...

MELCHIOR. And when your girls reached the proper age it would be exactly the same with them! Not that a girl is quite ... there's obviously no telling exactly what ... still, it's reasonable to assume ... and you can count on curiosity to play its part as well!

MORITZ. One question, by the way —

MELCHIOR. Yes?

MORITZ. You sure you'll answer?

MELCHIOR. Of course!

MORITZ. Promise?!

MELCHIOR. Cross my heart. — — Yes, Moritz?

MORITZ. Have you done the essay yet?

MELCHIOR. Come on, spit it out! — Nobody's listening, nobody can see us.

MORITZ. It goes without saying that my children would have to be working all day, in the lawn and garden, or amusing themselves with games that entailed physical exertion. They would have to ride, climb, do gymnastics, and, above all, not sleep on soft beds at night like we do. We're terribly soft. — I don't think you dream at all if you sleep on a hard bed.

MELCHIOR. From now until after the harvest I'm not sleeping on anything but my hammock. I put my bed behind the stove. It folds up. — Last winter I had a dream where I whipped our Lolo until he couldn't move a single limb. That was the most horrible thing I've ever dreamed. — Why are you giving me that funny look?

MORITZ. Have you already been feeling them?

MELCHIOR. What?

MORITZ. How did you put it?

MELCHIOR. Masculine stirrings?

MORITZ. M — hm.

MELCHIOR. — I sure have!

MORITZ. Me too. — — — — — — — — — — — — — — —

MELCHIOR. It's been going on for quite a while, in fact! — Almost a year now.

MORITZ. It hit me like a bolt of lightning.

MELCHIOR. You'd been dreaming?

MORITZ. But only very briefly … about some legs in turquoise tights that were trying — it's more accurate to say I *thought* they were trying — to climb over the podium at school. — I only saw them for a second.

MELCHIOR. George Zirschnitz dreamed about his *mother.*

MORITZ. He told you that?

MELCHIOR. Over on Gallows Hill!

MORITZ. If you knew what I've suffered since that night!

MELCHIOR. Pangs of guilt?

MORITZ. Pangs of guilt? — — — *Fear of death!*

MELCHIOR. Good Lord …

MORITZ. I thought I was incurable. I thought I was suffering from some internal injury. — The only thing that finally calmed me down was when I started to write my memoirs. Yes, yes, my dear Melchior, the last three weeks were a Gethsemane for me.

MELCHIOR. When it happened to me, I was more or less prepared for it. I felt a little ashamed. — But that was all.

MORITZ. And you're almost a full year younger than me, too!

MELCHIOR. That, Moritz, I wouldn't worry about. To the best of my knowledge there's no definite age limit for the first appearance of these phantoms. You know the big Lämmermeier kid with the straw-blond hair and the hook nose? He's three years older than

21

me. According to Hansy Rilow, he still doesn't dream about anything but sponge cake and apricot jelly.

MORITZ. Oh, please. How can Hansy Rilow know a thing like that?

MELCHIOR. He asked him.

MORITZ. He asked him? — I wouldn't dare ask anybody.

MELCHIOR. You asked me.

MORITZ. God, you're right. — It's possible that Hansy already had his will drawn up. — Truly a strange game they play with us. And we're supposed to be grateful! I don't remember ever feeling a longing for this kind of emotional turmoil. Why couldn't they have let me sleep in peace until everything was quiet again? My dear parents could have had a hundred better children than me. And now I've come, I don't know how, and I'm supposed to be responsible for not having stayed away. — Haven't you ever wondered yourself, Melchior, how we actually landed in this whirlpool?

MELCHIOR. You mean you still don't know, Moritz?

MORITZ. How can I be expected to know? — I see how chickens lay eggs, and I hear that supposedly my mother carried me "under her heart." But is that all there is to it? — I can also remember that even when I was five years old I was embarrassed whenever someone turned up the Queen of Hearts, with her décolletage. I don't get that feeling anymore. But now there's hardly a girl I can talk to without thinking something abominable, and — I swear to you, Melchior — I don't know *what*.

MELCHIOR. I'll tell you all about it. — I've gotten some of it from books, some of it from illustrations, and some of it from my observations of nature. You'll be surprised; it immediately made an atheist of me. I told George Zirschnitz, too! George Zirschnitz wanted to tell Hansy Rilow, but Hansy Rilow had already learned it all from his governess when he was little.

MORITZ. I went through *Meyer's Abridged* from A to Z. Words — nothing but words and words! Not one single straightforward explanation. Oh, this sense of shame! — What's the use of an encyclopedia that doesn't answer the most obvious question about life?

MELCHIOR. Have you ever seen two dogs running across the street?

MORITZ. No! — — You'd better not tell me anything today, Melchior. I still have Central America and Louis the Fifteenth hanging over my head. Plus the sixty lines of Homer, the seven equations, the Latin paper — I'd be falling on my butt all day again tomorrow. The only way I know how to grind is to be as dull as an ox.

MELCHIOR. Just come back to my room with me. In forty-five minutes I'll have the Homer, the equations, and *two* papers. I'll mix a couple of minor mistakes into yours, and you're all set. Mama will make us some more lemonade, and we'll have a nice cozy talk about reproduction.

MORITZ. I can't. — I can't have nice cozy talks about reproduction! If you want to do me a favor, you can give me your information in writing. Write down everything you know for me. Make it as short and clear as you can and stick it in between my books during gym tomorrow. I'll take it home without knowing I have it. At some point I'll come across it unexpectedly. I'll have no choice but to glance through it, with a weary eye ... If it's absolutely unavoidable you might also add a couple of illustrations.

MELCHIOR. You're like a girl. — Anything you say, though! It's the only work that completely interests me. — — One question, Moritz.

MORITZ. Hm?

MELCHIOR. — Have you ever seen a girl?

MORITZ. Yes!

MELCHIOR. Completely, though?

MORITZ. *Totally!*

MELCHIOR. So have I! — Illustrations won't be necessary, then.

MORITZ. During the shooting matches, in Leilich's Anatomical Museum! If I'd been caught, they would have thrown me out of school. — As pretty as the light of day, and — oh, so lifelike!

MELCHIOR. Last summer I was with Mama in Frankfurt. — You're leaving already, Moritz?

MORITZ. I've got homework. — Good night.

MELCHIOR. See you later.

Scene 3

Thea, Wendla, and Martha are coming up the street arm in arm.

MARTHA. The way the water gets in your shoes!

WENDLA. The way the wind whistles around your cheeks!

THEA. The way your heart pounds!

WENDLA. Let's go out to the bridge! Ilse said the river's full of trees and bushes. The boys have a raft on the water. I heard Melchi Gabor almost drowned last night.

THEA. Oh, he can swim!

MARTHA. You can say that again, girl!

WENDLA. If he couldn't swim, he'd have drowned for sure!

THEA. Your braid's coming out, Martha; your braid's coming out!

MARTHA. So? Let it come out! It annoys me every hour of the day. I can't wear my hair short like you, I can't wear it loose like Wendla, I can't have bangs, even at home I have to keep it up — all because of my aunts!

WENDLA. I'll bring some scissors to confirmation class tomorrow. You can be saying, "Blessed is the man who walks not in the counsel of the wicked," and I'll cut it off.

MARTHA. For God's sake, Wendla! Papa will beat me to a pulp and Mama will lock me in the coal cellar for three nights.

WENDLA. What does he hit you with, Martha?

MARTHA. Sometimes I think they'd feel something was missing if they didn't have a nasty little brat like me.

THEA. Now, now, now.

MARTHA. Weren't you allowed to run a sky-blue ribbon through the yoke of your chemise?

THEA. Pink satin! Mama says pink looks good on me with my pitch-black eyes.

MARTHA. Blue looked so cute on me! — Mama dragged me out of bed by my braids. I fell on the floor with my hands out — like this. — You see, Mama prays with us every night …

WENDLA. If I were you, I would have run away a long time ago.

24

MARTHA. "There you have it! That's what she's up to! — There you have it! — But we'll see about that — oh, we'll see about that! — At least she'll never have her mother to blame ... "

THEA. Hoo — Hoo —

MARTHA. Can you imagine what Mama meant by that, Thea?

THEA. Not me. — You, Wendla?

WENDLA. I would have just asked her.

MARTHA. I lay on the floor and screamed and howled. Then Papa comes in. *Rrrrip!* — off comes my chemise. I'm out the door. "There you have it! She wants to go out on the street like that now ... "

WENDLA. That can't be true, Martha.

MARTHA. I was freezing. I opened the door. I had to sleep in a gunnysack all night.

THEA. I couldn't sleep in a sack to save my life!

WENDLA. I'd be very happy to sleep in your sack for you sometime.

MARTHA. As long as a person doesn't get beaten.

THEA. But you could suffocate in there!

MARTHA. Your head stays out. The sack gets tied under your chin.

THEA. And then they beat you?

MARTHA. No. Only if there's something special.

WENDLA. What do they hit you with, Martha?

MARTHA. With, I don't know — all sorts of things. — Does *your* mother think it's indecent to eat a slice of bread in bed?

WENDLA. No, no.

MARTHA. I can't help thinking that they do have their fun — even if they never talk about it. — When I have children, I'm going to let them grow up like the weeds in our flower garden. Nobody pays any attention to them, and they're so tall, so thick — and meanwhile the roses on their stakes, in their planting boxes, get scrawnier every summer.

THEA. When I have children I'm going to dress them all in pink. Pink hats, pink skirts, pink shoes. Only the stockings — stockings black as night! Then when I go out for a walk I'll have them march along in front of me. — What about you, Wendla?

WENDLA. So you already know you're going to have some?

THEA. Why shouldn't we have some?

MARTHA. It's true that Aunt Euphemia doesn't have any.

THEA. Because she isn't *married,* you stupid goose!

25

WENDLA. My Aunt Bauer was married three times and didn't have a single one.

MARTHA. What would you want, Wendla, if you had some? Boys or girls?

WENDLA. Boys! Boys!

THEA. I want boys, too!

MARTHA. Me too. Better twenty boys than three girls.

THEA. Girls are boring!

MARTHA. If I hadn't turned out to be a girl, I definitely wouldn't want to become one now.

WENDLA. I think that's a matter of taste, Martha! Every day I think how happy I am to be a girl. Believe me, I wouldn't trade places with the son of a king. — But that's why I only want boys!

THEA. That's ridiculous, completely ridiculous, Wendla!

WENDLA. But surely it must be a thousand times more uplifting to be loved by a man than by a girl!

THEA. You can't possibly mean to say the assistant forest commissioner loves Melitta more than she loves him!

WENDLA. That's exactly what I mean, Thea! — Pfälle is proud. Pfälle is proud of being the assistant forest commissioner — because Pfälle doesn't have anything. — Melitta is *blissful,* because what she gets is ten thousand times more than what she is.

MARTHA. Aren't you proud of yourself, Wendla?

WENDLA. That would be silly.

MARTHA. How proud I'd be if I were you.

THEA. Just look at the way she puts her feet down — the way she looks straight ahead — the way she carries herself, Martha! — If that isn't pride!

WENDLA. But why?! I'm just so happy I'm a girl; if I wasn't a girl, I'd kill myself, so that next time ... *(Melchior passes by and waves to them.)*

THEA. He has a wonderful head.

MARTHA. That's how I picture the young Alexander when he was studying with Aristotle.

THEA. My God, Greek history. All I can remember is how Socrates was lying in a barrel when Alexander sold him the ass's shadow.

WENDLA. They say he's number three in his class.

THEA. Professor Brockenbohn says he could be number one if he wanted to.

MARTHA. He's got a nice forehead, but his friend has more soulful eyes.

THEA. Moritz Stiefel? — Of all the dopes!

MARTHA. I've always gotten along very well with him.

THEA. Every time you come near him, he makes you look like an idiot. At the children's ball the Rilows gave, he offered me some chocolates. Wendla, imagine, they were all soft and warm. Isn't that…? — He said he'd had them in his pocket too long.

WENDLA. Imagine this, Melchi Gabor told me at that party that there's nothing he believes in anymore — not God, not a hereafter — nothing in the world at all.

Scene 4

The park in front of the school. Melchior, Otto, George, Robert, Hansy Rilow, Lämmermeier.

MELCHIOR. Do any of you know where Moritz Stiefel is?

GEORGE. He's in trouble! Boy, is he in trouble!

OTTO. Kids that play with matches get their fingers burned!

LÄMMERMEIER. I sure as hell wouldn't want to be where he is now!

ROBERT. The shamelessness! — The incredible gall!

MELCHIOR. Wh — Wh — What are you talking about?

GEORGE. What are we talking about? — Hey. I'll tell you…!

LÄMMERMEIER. I don't want to be the one who talked.

OTTO. Me neither — no way!

MELCHIOR. I'm giving you five seconds …

ROBERT. Simply put: Moritz Stiefel got into the *conference room.*

MELCHIOR. The conference room…?

OTTO. The conference room! — Right after Latin.

GEORGE. He was the last one out; he hung back on purpose.

LÄMMERMEIER. I was halfway around the corner when I saw him open the door.

MELCHIOR. The hell you say!

LÄMMERMEIER. He'll be lucky not to land in hell himself!

GEORGE. The administration must have left the key in the door.

ROBERT. Or Moritz Stiefel has a skeleton key.

OTTO. I wouldn't put it past him.

LÄMMERMEIER. He'll get at least detention.

ROBERT. And a note on his report card!

OTTO. If it's not already full of F's.

HANSY. There he is!

MELCHIOR. White as a sheet. *(Moritz enters in extreme agitation.)*

LÄMMERMEIER. Moritz, Moritz, what have you done!

MORITZ. — — Nothing — nothing — —

ROBERT. You're feverish!

MORITZ. — with happiness — with bliss — with jubilation —

OTTO. They caught you?

MORITZ. I passed! — Melchior, I passed: — Oh, now the world can end! — I passed! — Who would have believed I'd pass! — I read it twenty times! — I can't believe it — sweet God, it was still there! It was still there! *I passed!* — *(Smiling.)* I don't know — I feel so strange — the ground is spinning ... Melchior, Melchior, if you knew what I've been through!

HANSY. Congratulations, Moritz. — Just be glad you got away with it.

MORITZ. You don't know, Hansy, you have *no idea* what was at stake. For three weeks I've been sneaking past that door like it's the gates of hell. Then today I notice it's ajar. I think if you'd offered me a million — nothing, *nothing* could have stopped me! — I'm standing in the middle of the room — I open up the file — turn the pages — find it — — and the whole time ... It makes me shiver —

MELCHIOR. ... And the whole time?

MORITZ. And the whole time the door's wide open behind me. — How I got out of there ... how I made it down the stairs, I have no idea.

HANSY. — Did Ernst Röbel pass, too?

MORITZ. Yes, indeed, Hansy. Yes, indeed! — Ernst Röbel also passed.

ROBERT. Then you can't have read it right. Not counting the idiots, there's sixty-one of us including you and Röbel, and the classroom upstairs doesn't hold more than sixty.

MORITZ. I read it perfectly right. Ernst Röbel's getting moved up the same as me — both of us *provisionally*, of course, to begin with. During the first quarter they'll see which of us has to make way for the other. — Poor Röbel! — God knows I'm not worried about myself anymore. I've been too close to the edge now for that.

OTTO. I bet you five marks you don't make it.

MORITZ. You're broke. I don't want to wipe you out. — From now on, I'm going to grind like hell! — I can say it now — you can take it or leave it — nothing matters now — I — I know how true it is: If I hadn't passed, I would have shot myself.

ROBERT. Show-off!

GEORGE. Chicken!

OTTO. I wish I'd been there to see it!

LÄMMERMEIER. What do you want to bet — a sock in the mouth?

MELCHIOR. *(Gives him one.)* — — Come on, Moritz. Let's go to the ranger's hut.

GEORGE. You mean you believe that drivel?

MELCHIOR. What's it to you? — — Let them talk, Moritz! Go, let's go, let's get out of town! *(Professor Starver and Professor Brockenbohn pass by.)*

BROCKENBOHN. That the best of my pupils can be attracted precisely to the very worst, my dear colleague, is incomprehensible to me.

STARVER. To me as well, my dear colleague.

Scene 5

A sunny afternoon. Melchior and Wendla meet in the woods.

MELCHIOR. Is it really you, Wendla? — What are you doing up here by yourself? — I've been roving all over the woods for three hours without meeting a soul, and now suddenly I see you coming out of the thickest underbrush!

WENDLA. Yes, it's me.

MELCHIOR. If I didn't know you were Wendla Bergmann, I'd think you were a dryad fallen from the boughs.

WENDLA. No, no, I'm Wendla Bergmann. — Where did you come from?

MELCHIOR. I've been pursuing my thoughts.

WENDLA. I'm looking for woodruff. Mama wants to make May punch. At first she wanted to come along herself, but Aunt Bauer showed up at the last minute, and she doesn't like climbing. — So I came up here by myself.

MELCHIOR. Do you have your woodruff yet?

WENDLA. The basket's full of it. Over there under the beech trees it's thick as clover. — As a matter of fact, I'm looking for a way out now. I seem to have gotten turned around. Do you happen to know what time it is?

MELCHIOR. It's just three-thirty. — When are they expecting you?

WENDLA. I thought it was later. I lay for a long time in the moss by the creek, and dreamed. Time passed so quickly; I was afraid it would be getting on toward evening.

MELCHIOR. If they aren't expecting you yet, let's rest here a little longer. Under the oak tree there is my favorite spot. If you lean your head back against the trunk and stare at the sky through the branches, you get hypnotized. The ground is still warm from the morning sun. — There's something I've been wanting to ask you for weeks, Wendla.

WENDLA. I have to be home by five, though.

MELCHIOR. We'll go together. I'll carry your basket and we'll take the path through the ravine. In ten minutes we'll be on the bridge! — When you lie here like this, with your forehead in your hands, you have the strangest thoughts ... *(The two of them settle down under the oak tree.)*

WENDLA. What did you want to ask me, Melchior?

MELCHIOR. I've heard, Wendla, that you often visit poor people. That you bring them food, and clothes and money, too. Do you do this out of your own free will, or does your mother send you?

WENDLA. Usually my mother sends me. It's poor worker families with scads of children. A lot of times the husband can't find work, so they're cold and hungry. At home we have all kinds of old stuff lying around in closets and dressers that doesn't get used anymore. But what made you think of it?

MELCHIOR. When your mother sends you places like that, do you like to go, or not?

WENDLA. Oh, I love to go! How can you ask!

MELCHIOR. But the children are dirty, the women are sick, the rooms are full of trash, the men hate you because you don't work ...

WENDLA. That's not true, Melchior. And if it were true, I'd go there all the sooner!

MELCHIOR. What do you mean, all the sooner?

WENDLA. I'd go there all the sooner. — It would make me even happier to be able to help them.

MELCHIOR. So it's for your own pleasure that you visit poor people?

WENDLA. I visit them because they're poor.

MELCHIOR. But if it didn't make you happy, you wouldn't go?

WENDLA. Can I help it if it makes me happy?

MELCHIOR. And yet for this you're supposed to go to heaven! — Which means this thing that's been keeping me awake every night for a month now is true! — Can a miser help it if visiting sick, dirty children doesn't make him happy?

WENDLA. Oh, I'm sure it would make you happier than anything!

MELCHIOR. And yet for this he's supposed to die an eternal death! — I'm going to write a treatise and send it to Reverend Bleekhead. He's the cause of all this. The trash he feeds us about the joy of *self-sacrifice!* — If he can't give me an answer, I'll stop going to Sunday school and I won't get confirmed.

WENDLA. Why make things miserable for your mother and father? Just get confirmed; it's not going to kill you. If there weren't those awful white dresses for us and those trooper pants for you, a person might even be able to get excited about it.

MELCHIOR. There's no such thing as sacrifice! There's no such thing as selflessness! — I watch the good people enjoying the warmth of their hearts, I watch the bad people trembling and groaning — I watch you, Wendla Bergmann, shaking your curls and laughing, and it makes me feel as stone sober as an outcast. — — What were you dreaming about, Wendla, when you were lying in the grass by the creek?

WENDLA. — — Stupid things — foolish things —

MELCHIOR. With your eyes open?!

WENDLA. I dreamed I was a poor, poor beggar girl, I was sent out in the street at five in the morning, I had to beg from rude, hard-hearted people all day long, in storms and bad weather. And if I came home at night, shivering with cold and hunger, and I didn't have as much money as my father expected, I'd get beaten — beaten —

MELCHIOR. I know this kind of thing, Wendla. You have those

silly children's books to thank for it. Believe me, people as brutal as that don't exist anymore.

WENDLA. But they do, Melchior, you're wrong. — Martha Bessel gets beaten every night, and you can see the welts the next day. Oh, what that girl must suffer! Your face gets burning hot when you hear her tell about it. I feel so horribly sorry for her, sometimes I have to cry in my pillow in the middle of the night. I've been trying for months to figure out how to help her. — I'd be happy to take her place for a whole week sometime.

MELCHIOR. Her father should be reported immediately. They'd take the child away from him.

WENDLA. I, Melchior, have never in my life been beaten — not one single time. I can hardly imagine how it feels to be beaten. I've tried beating myself to see what it does to you. — It must be a dreadful feeling.

MELCHIOR. I don't think a child is ever improved by it.

WENDLA. Improved by what?

MELCHIOR. By being beaten.

WENDLA. — With this stick, for example! — Hoo, it's so tough and thin.

MELCHIOR. You'd draw blood with that.

WENDLA. Would you hit me with it once?

MELCHIOR. Who?

WENDLA. Me.

MELCHIOR. What's gotten into you, Wendla?

WENDLA. What's wrong with it?

MELCHIOR. Just calm down! — I'm not going to hit you.

WENDLA. But if I let you!

MELCHIOR. Never!

WENDLA. But if I ask you to, Melchior!

MELCHIOR. Are you out of your mind?

WENDLA. I've never been beaten in my whole life!

MELCHIOR. If you can ask for a thing like that…!

WENDLA. — Please — please —

MELCHIOR. I'll teach you to ask! — *(He hits her.)*

WENDLA. Oh God — I don't feel a thing!

MELCHIOR. Of course not — — through all your skirts …

WENDLA. Well, hit my legs then!

MELCHIOR. Wendla! — *(He hits her harder.)*

WENDLA. You're just patting me! — You're patting me!

MELCHIOR. Wait, you witch, I'll whip that Satan right out of you! *(Melchior throws the switch aside and flies at her with his fists so violently that she bursts into a terrible scream. He pays no attention, but thrashes her as if enraged, while thick tears run down his cheeks. Suddenly he jumps up, clutches his temples with both hands, and plunges into the woods, sobbing piteously from the depths of his soul.)*

End of Act One

ACT TWO

Scene 1

Evening in Melchior's study. The window is open, the lamp on the table is lit. Melchior and Moritz on the sofa.

MORITZ. I'm in good spirits again, just a little bit stirred up. — During Greek, though, I was sleeping like a drunken Polyphemus. I'm amazed that old Fitztongue didn't tweak my ears. — I came within an inch of being late this morning. — The first thing I thought of when I woke up was the verbs in μι. — Christ-hell-god-damn it, I conjugated all through breakfast and all the way to school until I was ready to throw up. — It must have been just after three when I dozed off. The pen made another blot in my book. When Mathilda woke me up, my lamp was smoking and the blackbirds in the elder bushes outside my window sounded so happy to be alive — I immediately started feeling unspeakably melancholy again. I put on my collar and dragged a brush through my hair. — — But it feels good when you've accomplished something in spite of yourself.
MELCHIOR. Can I roll you a cigarette?
MORITZ. Thanks, I don't smoke. — If I can only keep it up! I'm going to work and work until my eyes pop out of my head. — Ernst Röbel's already failed six times since spring vacation; three times in Greek, twice in Brockenbohn's class; and the last time in literature. I myself have only been in that deplorable position five times; and from now on it's not going to happen at all! — Röbel won't shoot himself. Röbel doesn't have parents who are sacrificing everything for him. Whenever he wants to, he can go be a soldier, or a cowboy, or a sailor. If *I* flunk out, my father will have a stroke and my mother will end up in the loony bin. A person couldn't survive a thing like that! — Before the exam, I prayed to God to give me tuberculosis and let me off the hook. And I got off it — although even now I can sense it hanging in the distance, with a

34

glimmering around it that makes me scared to raise my eyes, day and night. — But now that I'm on the ladder I'll keep on climbing. My guarantee is the logical certainty that I can't fall without breaking my neck.

MELCHIOR. There's an unexpected nastiness to life. I could see hanging myself in a tree. — What's taking Mama with the tea!

MORITZ. Your tea will do me good, Melchior! Honestly, I'm shaking. I feel so peculiarly outside of myself. Touch me, would you please. I see — I hear — I feel things much more clearly — and yet everything's so dreamlike — oh, so atmospheric. — The way the lawn stretches out in the moonlight there, so quiet, so deep, as if it reached into eternity. — Figures veiled in crepe come out of the bushes and scurry in breathless haste across the glades, and vanish in the twilight. It feels like there's going to be a council meeting under the chestnut tree. — Maybe we should go down there, Melchior?

MELCHIOR. Let's wait till we've had our tea.

MORITZ. The leaves are whispering so busily. — It's as if I was hearing my grandmother sit back and tell the story of *The Queen without a Head*. — There was a fabulously beautiful queen, as beautiful as the sun, more beautiful than all the maidens in the land. Only, unfortunately, she'd been born without a head. She couldn't eat, couldn't drink, couldn't see or laugh or kiss. The only way she could communicate with her court was with her small white hands. With her elegant little feet she tapped out death sentences and declarations of war. Then one day she was conquered by a king who happened to have two heads, which were always getting in each other's hair and arguing so frantically that neither of them could get a word in edgewise. The chief wizard of the court took the smaller of the two and put it on the queen. And lo and behold, it fit her perfectly. Whereupon the king married the queen, and instead of getting in each other's hair the two of them kissed each other on the forehead, on the cheeks, and mouth, and lived happily ever after ... What garbage! Since the end of vacation I haven't been able to get that headless queen out of my head. Whenever I see a pretty girl I see her without a head — and then suddenly it seems like I'm a headless queen myself ... Sometime maybe someone will put another head on me. *(Mrs. Gabor comes in with the steaming tea, which she puts on the table in front of Moritz and Melchior.)*

MRS. GABOR. Here, kids, I hope you enjoy it. Hello, Mr. Stiefel;

how are you?

MORITZ. Thank you, Mrs. Gabor. — I'm listening to the dance down there.

MRS. GABOR. You don't look at all well, though! — Are you feeling all right?

MORITZ. It's nothing. I've been going to bed on the late side the last few nights.

MELCHIOR. Can you imagine, he was up all night studying.

MRS. GABOR. You shouldn't do things like that, Mr. Stiefel. You should take care of yourself. Don't neglect your health. School is no substitute for good health. — Take brisk walks in the fresh air! That's worth more at your age than memorizing Virgil.

MORITZ. I'll take brisk walks in the fresh air. You're right. You can do your exercises while you're exercising too. Why didn't I think of that myself! — But I'd still have to do the written work at home.

MELCHIOR. You can do the written stuff here with me; it'll make it easier for both of us. — You know, don't you, Mama, that Max von Trenk came down with brain fever! — At lunchtime today Hansy Rilow came straight from Trenk's deathbed to tell Mr. Hart-Payne that Trenk had just died while he was with him. — "Well?" says Hart-Payne. "Don't you still have two hours of detention to do from last week? Here's the slip for the custodian. I want this matter straightened out once and for all! The entire class will participate in the funeral." — Hansy was stunned.

MRS. GABOR. What book do you have there, Melchior?

MELCHIOR. *Faust.*

MRS. GABOR. Have you read it yet?

MELCHIOR. Not all of it.

MORITZ. Right now we're doing the Walpurgis Night.

MRS. GABOR. If I were you, I would have waited another year or two.

MELCHIOR. Mama, I can't think of any book where I've found so many great things. Why shouldn't I read it?

MRS. GABOR. — Because you don't understand it.

MELCHIOR. You have no way of knowing, Mama. I'm fully aware that I'm not in a position to appreciate the work in all its sublimity ...

MORITZ. We always read together; it greatly facilitates our comprehension!

MRS. GABOR. Melchior, you're old enough to know what's good for you and what's bad for you. Do whatever you think you can justify to yourself. I'll be the very first to express my gratitude if you never give me any reason to have to deny you something. — I just wanted to call your attention to the fact that even the best things can have harmful effects if a person is not yet equipped with the maturity to properly appreciate them. — I will always prefer to place my trust in *you,* rather than in any given educational method. — — If you need anything else, kids, you can come out and call me, Melchior. I'll be in my bedroom. *(Mrs. Gabor exits.)*

MORITZ. — Your mama meant the business with Gretchen.

MELCHIOR. Did we spend even one minute talking about that?

MORITZ. Faust himself couldn't have dismissed it more cold-bloodedly!

MELCHIOR. After all, as a work of art, the play doesn't culmi-nate in that one act of infamy! — Faust could have promised to marry the girl and then abandoned her; in my eyes he wouldn't have been the tiniest bit less guilty. As far as I'm concerned, Gretchen could have died of a broken heart. — When you see how convulsively everybody always latches onto that one part, you'd think the whole world revolves around penis and vagina!

MORITZ. To tell you the truth, Melchior, that's exactly the impression I've had since I read your essay. — It fell on the floor at the beginning of vacation. I'd picked up the *Survey of World History.* — I locked the door and raced through the flickering lines the way a frightened owl flies through a burning forest — I think I read most of it with my eyes closed. Your explanations sounded to me like a series of vague memories, like a song a person used to sing to himself when he was little, and then hears again when he's just about to die and it comes out of someone else's mouth and breaks his heart. — The thing that affected me the most was what you wrote about girls. I can't get it out of my mind. Believe me, Melchior, it's sweeter to have to suffer a wrong than to commit one. To have to submit to such a sweet wrong without deserving it seems to me the essence of all earthly bliss.

MELCHIOR. I don't want my bliss to come as charity!

MORITZ. Why not?

MELCHIOR. I don't *want* anything I haven't had to fight for!

MORITZ. But is it even pleasure then, Melchior? — A girl's pleas-ure, Melchior, is like the rapture of the gods. A girl's natural disposition makes her put up a fight. She keeps herself free from any kind of bitterness right until the last second, so she can suddenly be transported straight to heaven. A girl is still afraid of Hell at the very moment she feels a paradise blossoming. Her perceptions are as fresh as a spring that rises up out of rock. A girl takes hold of a chalice that earthly lips have never touched before, a cup of nectar that flames and sparkles as she drains it ... I imagine the satisfaction that a man gets out of this is stale and flat.

MELCHIOR. Imagine it however you want, but keep it to yourself. — I don't like to imagine it ...

Scene 2

The living room.

MRS. BERGMANN. *(Her hat on, her cape around her shoulders, a basket on her arm, enters, beaming, through the middle door.)* Wendla! — Wendla!

WENDLA. *(Appears in her little slip and bodice at the side door right.)* What is it, Mother?

MRS. BERGMANN. You're up already, baby? — My, my, isn't that nice of you!

WENDLA. You've already been out?

MRS. BERGMANN. Hurry up and get dressed! — You have to run over to Ina's right away, you have to take this basket to her!

WENDLA. *(Getting fully dressed during the following.)* You were at Ina's? — How is Ina? — Still no better?

MRS. BERGMANN. Just think, Wendla, the stork came last night and brought her a little baby boy.

WENDLA. A boy? — A boy — Oh, that's wonderful — — That explains the never-ending influenza!

MRS. BERGMANN. A splendid little boy!

WENDLA. I have to see him, Mother! — Now I'm an aunt for the third time — the aunt of a girl and two boys!

MRS. BERGMANN. And what boys they are! — That's what happens when you live right under the eaves of the church. — It'll only be two years ago tomorrow that she came down the aisle in her muslin dress.

WENDLA. Were you there when he brought him?

MRS. BERGMANN. He'd just flown away again. — Don't you want to pin a rose on your dress?

WENDLA. Why didn't you get there a little earlier, Mother?

MRS. BERGMANN. I've got a feeling he brought you something too — a brooch or something.

WENDLA. It's really too bad!

MRS. BERGMANN. That's what he did all right! He brought you a brooch!

WENDLA. I have enough brooches …

MRS. BERGMANN. Then, baby, be satisfied. What else do you want?

WENDLA. I'd have given anything to know whether he flew in through the window or down the chimney.

MRS. BERGMANN. That's something you'll have to ask Ina. Ha, that's something you'll have to ask Ina, darling. Ina will give you all the details. Ina talked to him for a full half hour.

WENDLA. I'll ask Ina when I go over there.

MRS. BERGMANN. And don't forget now, either, angel-face! I'd be interested to know myself whether he came in through the window or the chimney.

WENDLA. Or should I ask the chimney sweep instead? — A chimney sweep should know better than anyone else whether he flies through the chimney or not.

MRS. BERGMANN. Not the chimney sweep, baby; not the chimney sweep. What does a chimney sweep know about the stork! — He'd yakkety-yak to you about all sorts of humbug he doesn't even believe in himself … Wh — What are you gawking at in the street?

WENDLA. A man, Mother — three times bigger than an ox! — With feet like steamboats…!

MRS. BERGMANN. *(Rushing to the window.)* Not possible! — Not possible!

WENDLA. *(Simultaneously.)* He's got a bed frame under his chin and he's fiddling "The Watch on the Rhine" on it — He just went around the corner …

MRS. BERGMANN. You'll just never grow up, will you! — Scaring the life out of your dumb old mother! — Go put your hat on. I'll be surprised if you ever start showing good sense. — I've stopped hoping.

WENDLA. So have I, Mommy, so have I. — It's a sad thing about my good sense. — I have a sister who's been married for two and a half years, and I'm an aunt now for the third time myself, and I have absolutely no idea how it all happens … Don't get mad, Mommy; don't get mad! Who in the world am I supposed to ask if not you! Please, Mommy, tell me! Tell me, Mommy! I'm ashamed of myself. I'm begging you, Mother, say something! Don't tell me not to ask things like that. Answer me — what goes on? — how does it all happen? — You don't seriously expect me to keep on believing in the stork when I'm fourteen years old.

MRS. BERGMANN. Goodness gracious, what a strange little girl you are today! — These ideas you get! — I certainly can't do a thing like that!

WENDLA. Why not, Mother! — Why not! — It can't be anything too horrid if it makes everyone so happy!

MRS. BERGMANN. Oh — oh, God help me! — I'd deserve to be … Go get dressed, young lady; go get dressed!

WENDLA. I'm going … And if your baby goes out and asks the chimney sweep?

MRS. BERGMANN. It's enough to drive you mad! — Come here, baby, come here, I'll tell you all about it! I'll tell you everything … Merciful heavens! — But not today, Wendla! — Tomorrow, the day after tomorrow, next week … whenever you like, sweetheart.

WENDLA. Tell me today, Mother; tell me now! Right now! — Now that I've seen you so upset, I definitely won't be able to calm down unless you tell me.

MRS. BERGMANN. I can't, Wendla.

WENDLA. Oh, why can't you, Mommy! — Here, I'll kneel at your feet and put my head in your lap. You can cover my head with your apron and talk and talk like you're the only person in the room. I won't flinch; I won't scream; I'll stick it out patiently no matter what.

MRS. BERGMANN. — Heaven knows, Wendla, that I'm not to blame! Heaven is my witness! — Come, in the name of God! — I will tell you, my child, how you came into the world. — So listen carefully, Wendla …

WENDLA. *(Under her apron.)* I'm listening.

MRS. BERGMANN. *(Ecstatically.)* — Baby, it's just no use! — I can't take the responsibility! — I'd deserve to be put in jail — to have you taken away from me ...

WENDLA. *(Under her apron.)* Be brave, Mother!

MRS. BERGMANN. Listen to me, then ...

WENDLA. *(Under her apron, trembling.)* Oh God, oh God!

MRS. BERGMANN. In order to have a child — are you getting this, Wendla?

WENDLA. Quick, Mother — I can't stand it.

MRS. BERGMANN. — In order to have a child — you have to — *love* — the man — you're married to — *love him,* I tell you — in a way that you can only love a husband! You have to love him so much, *with all your heart and all your soul,* that — that it's impossible to describe! You have to *love* him, Wendla, in a way that you at your age absolutely can't ... Now you know.

WENDLA. *(Getting up.)* God — Almighty!

MRS. BERGMANN. Now you know the trials that lie in store for you!

WENDLA. — And that's all there is?

MRS. BERGMANN. So help me God! — — Now take the basket there and go over to Ina's. You'll get some hot chocolate and cake there too. — Come here, let's have another look at you — lace-up boots, silk gloves, sailor blouse, roses in your hair ..... but this little skirt is really getting much too short for you, Wendla!

WENDLA. Did you get some meat for lunch yet, Mommy?

MRS. BERGMANN. May the Lord bless you and keep you! — When I have a chance, I'll sew a ruffle on the bottom.

Scene 3

HANSY. *(Carrying a lamp, he bolts the door behind him and raises the lid.)* Have you prayed tonight, Desdemona? *(He pulls a reproduction of Palma Vecchio's* Venus *out from under his shirt.)* Our Father, who art in heaven? You don't look like it, my love — rapt in your expectation of what's coming, as in that sweet moment of budding ecstasy when I saw you lying in the window of Jonathan Schlesinger's — your supple legs and arms, the gentle curving of

41

your hips, your firm young breasts just as enticing now — oh, how delirious with joy the great master must have been when the fourteen-year-old original lay stretched out on the divan before his eyes! Will you still come to me in dreams now and then? — I'll welcome you with outstretched arms and kiss you till you're breathless. You'll move in with me like a royal heiress reclaiming her deserted palace. Gates and doors will open at the touch of unseen hands while, down in the park, the fountain will happily begin to splash … It is the cause! — It is the cause! — You can tell by the fearsome pounding in my breast that my motive for this murder isn't frivolous. My throat goes dry at the thought of the lonely nights ahead of me. I swear to you, my child, I'm not doing this because I've had too much of you. How could anyone admit to have gotten sick of *you?*

But you suck the marrow out of my bones, you bend my back, you steal the last sparkle from my youthful eyes. — You're too demanding in your inhuman diffidence, too exhausting with your unmoving limbs! — Either you or me! — And the victory is mine.

If I wanted to count them — all the departed with whom I've fought the same battle here! — : Thuman's *Psyche* — another legacy of the hatchet-faced Mademoiselle Angélique, that rattlesnake in the paradise of my childhood; Correggio's *Io*; Lossow's *Galatea*; then a cupid by Bouguereau; J. van Beer's *Ada*, whom I had to abduct from a secret compartment in Papa's desk in order to add her to my harem; a quivering, twitching *Leda* by Makart that I happened to find in my brother's lecture notes — *seven,* you pubescent candidate for death, have hurried down this path to Tartarus ahead of you! Let that be your consolation; leave off with these imploring looks, don't try to push my torments beyond the limits of endurance.

You're not dying for *your* sins, you're dying for *mine.* — In heartrending self-defense against my own incursions, I'm committing my seventh conjugal murder. There's something tragic in the role of Bluebeard. I think that all his murdered wives put together suffered less than he did each time he strangled one.

But my conscience will be pacified, my body will regain its strength when you, devil, no longer reside in the red satin cushions of my jewel box. In your place I'll invite Bodenhausen's *Lurlei* or Linger's *Forsaken Maiden* or Defregger's *Loni* to move into this sumptuous chamber of pleasure — which will add all the more speed to my recovery! Three more little months, perhaps, and your unveiled *Jehoshaphat*, sweet soul, would have begun to eat away my poor brain the way the sun consumes a lump of butter. It's high time we untied the knot.

Brr, there's a Heliogabalus in me! *Moritura me salutat!* — Girl, girl, why do you press your knees together? — Why even now? — — Are you mindful of inscrutable eternity? — *One* twitch, and I'll set you free! — *One* feminine gesture, *one* sign of lust, of sympathy, girl! — I'll frame you in gold and hang you above my bed! — Don't you see that it's your *chasteness* alone that gives birth to my debaucheries? — Woe, woe unto those who are inhuman!

... One never fails to notice that she's had an exemplary upbringing. — *Well, so have I.*

My heart is breaking — — nonsense! — Even Saint Agnes died for her restraint, and she wasn't half as naked as you! — One last kiss on your blossoming body, the childishly budding breast — your sweetly rounded — your horribly cruel knee ...

Have you prayed tonight, Desdemona? It is the cause, it is the cause, my soul. *Let me not name it to you, you chaste stars!* It is the cause! — *(The picture falls into the depths; he lowers the lid.)*

Scene 4

A hayloft. Melchior is lying on his back in the fresh hay. Wendla comes up the ladder.

WENDLA. *This* is where you've been hiding? — Everyone's looking for you. The wagon's gone back out again. You have to help. There's a storm coming up.
MELCHIOR. Get away from me! — Get away from me!
WENDLA. What's wrong? — What are you hiding your face for?
MELCHIOR. Go away, go away! — I'm going to throw you down the ladder.
WENDLA. In that case I'm definitely not going. — *(Drops to her knees by him.)* Why won't you come out in the field with us, Melchior? — It's dark and muggy in here. What do *we* care if we get soaked to the skin!

MELCHIOR. The hay has such a wonderful smell. — The sky out there must be as black as the cloth on a coffin. — All I can see is the glowing poppy on your breast — and I can hear your heart beating —

WENDLA. — Don't kiss me, Melchior! — Don't kiss me!

MELCHIOR. — I can hear your heart — beating —

WENDLA. — People love each other — if they kiss — — — Don't, don't — —

MELCHIOR. Oh, believe me, there's no such thing as *love!* — There's only selfishness, only ego! — I love you as little as you love me. —

WENDLA. — — Don't — — — — — — — — — — Don't, Melchior! — —

MELCHIOR. — — — Wendla!

WENDLA. Oh, Melchior! — — — — — — don't — — don't — —

Scene 5

MRS. GABOR. *(Sits, writes.)* Dear Mr. Stiefel: For twenty-four hours I have considered and reconsidered everything you wrote to me, and it's with a heavy heart that I now take up my pen. To provide you with the cost of a passage to America will — I give you my most solemn assurance — *not* be possible. In the first place, I don't have a sum like that at my disposal, and in the second place, even if I did have it, it would be the most grievous sin imaginable to furnish you with the means of committing such a rash and fateful act. You would be doing me a bitter injustice, Mr. Stiefel, if you were to see in my refusal a sign of insufficient love. On the contrary, it would be the most gross violation of my duty as a motherly friend if I were to allow your momentary distress to cause me to lose my own head as well and blindly yield to my immediate impulses in this situation. I'm fully prepared — should you so desire — to write to your parents. I will try to convince your parents that in the course of this term you did as much as you were able to, that you have exhausted your strength to the point where a strict judgment on your abilities would not only be unjustified but indeed would have the most detrimental of effects upon your spiritual and physical well-being.

Your veiled threat to take your own life, should I not make it possible for you to run away, did quite frankly, Mr. Stiefel, put me off somewhat. No matter how undeserved one's misfortunes may be, one should never, ever allow oneself to be driven to choose underhanded methods. The way in which you would make me, who has shown you nothing but kindness, responsible for a potential atrocity, smacks of something that a *mean-spirited* person could all too easily construe as an extortion attempt. I must confess that this behavior is the very last thing I would have expected from you, who in all else is so well aware of one's duty to oneself. However, I'm firmly convinced that you were still too much under the influence of your initial fright to be fully conscious of what you were doing.

And so I trust that these words of mine will find you already in a more composed frame of mind. Accept matters as they stand. In my opinion, it is wholly impermissible to judge a young man by his report card. We have too many examples of very poor students who grew up to be excellent people and, vice versa, of outstanding students who acquitted themselves rather indifferently in life. In any case you have my assurance that your misfortune will not, insofar as it lies in my power, in any way affect your intercourse with Melchior. It will continue to be a joy to see my son in the company of someone who, no matter how the world may judge him, was able to win my fullest sympathy.

So chin up, Mr. Stiefel! — Similar crises of one kind or another befall each and every one of us and simply have to be survived. If everyone immediately resorted to dagger and poison, the world might soon run out of people. Hoping to hear from you again soon, with the very best wishes from your unswervingly devoted motherly friend, Fanny G.

Scene 6

The Bergmanns' garden in morning sunshine.

WENDLA. Why did you sneak out of the room? — To look for violets! — Because Mother sees me smiling. — Why can't you make your lips work anymore? — I don't know. — I *don't know*, I can't find the words ... The path is like a thick carpet — no pebbles, no thorns. — My feet don't touch the ground ... Oh, did I sleep last night! This is where they were. — I'm starting to feel as serious as a nun at communion. — Sweet violets! — Shush, Mommy. I'm ready to put my sackcloth on. — Oh God, if only somebody would come who I could throw my arms around and talk to.

Scene 7

Dusk. A few clouds are in the sky, the path winds through low brush and reeds. The river can be heard murmuring at some distance.

MORITZ. Better safe than sorry. — I don't fit in. Let them climb up on each other's heads. — I'll pull the door shut behind me and set myself free. — I'm not all that keen on sticking around just to get sidestepped. I didn't force myself on them. Why should I force myself on them now! — I don't have any contract with the dear Lord. You can twist things around any way you like. They forced me. — I don't blame my parents. They had to have been prepared for the worst, though. They were old enough to know what they were doing. I was a baby when I came into the world — otherwise I might have been smart enough to become a different person. — Why should I have to suffer for the fact that everyone else was already here! I must have been dropped on my head … if someone gives me a mad dog for a present, I'll give the mad dog back to him. And if he won't take his mad dog back, I'll be humane and … I must have been dropped on my head! A person enters the world entirely by chance, and he shouldn't, after careful consideration — — — it's enough to make you shoot yourself!

— At least the weather showed some consideration. All day it looked like rain and now it's clearing up. — There's an unusual stillness out here. Nothing harsh or irritating anywhere. The sky and earth are like a transparent spiderweb. And everything seems so comfortable. The landscape is as pretty as a lullaby — "*go to sleep, go to sleep my little prince,*" like Miss Snandulia sang. Too bad she holds her elbows so ungraciously! — The last time I danced was at the Saint Cecilia's Day party. Snandulia only dances with eligible men. The silk gown she wore was cut low in the front and the back. In back it went down to her waist, and in front it went straight to my brain stem. — She couldn't have been wearing anything underneath …

— — — — — — — — — — — — — — That would be something that could still captivate me. — More for curiosity's sake. — It must be a strange sensation — a feeling like being swept over a waterfall — — — I won't tell anyone that I'm returning without having finished the job. I'll act like I experienced all that like everyone else … There's something shameful about having been a human being without ever getting to know the most human thing of all. — You come from *Egypt,* sir, and you haven't seen the *pyramids?!*

I don't want to cry again today. I don't want to think about my funeral again — — Melchior will lay a wreath on my coffin. Reverend Bleekhead will console my parents. Mr. Hart-Payne will cite some historical examples. — I probably won't get a gravestone. I would have liked to have a snow-white marble urn on a black granite column — fortunately I won't miss it. The monuments are for the living, not the dead.

I'd need a whole year to say goodbye to everybody in my head. I don't want to cry again. I'm glad to be able to look back without bitterness. All the wonderful evenings I spent with Melchior! — under the willows; at the ranger's hut; out there on the army road where the five linden trees are; up on the mountain in the ruins of the Runenberg. — — —

When the time comes, I'm going to concentrate as hard as I can on whipped cream. Whipped cream is so innocuous. It's filling and it leaves behind a pleasant aftertaste ... Human beings, too, I'd imagined as being infinitely worse. I never met anyone who didn't want the best from himself. There've been many people I've pitied for my sake.

I approach the altar like the youth in ancient Etruria whose death rattle buys his brothers a year's worth of health and happiness. — I drain the bitter cup and let the mysterious terrors of departure roll over my tongue. I sob with sorrow for my fate. — — Life has given me the cold shoulder. Earnest, friendly eyes are beckoning to me from the other side: the headless queen, the headless queen — sympathy waiting for me with soft arms ... Your commandments are for the immature; I carry my free ticket inside me. When the empty shell falls, the butterfly flutters away from it; the illusion is no longer an embarrassment. — It isn't fair of you to make me dizzy! The fog is clearing; life is a matter of taste.

ILSE. *(In worn-out clothes, a colorful scarf around her head, grabs him by the shoulder from behind.)* Lose something?

MORITZ. Ilse?!

ILSE. What are you looking for out here?

MORITZ. Why did you scare me like that?

ILSE. What are you looking for? — Did you lose something?

MORITZ. What did you scare me so horribly for?

ILSE. I was in the city. I'm on my way home.

MORITZ. I don't know what I lost.

ILSE. No point in looking for it, then.

MORITZ. Damn it, damn it, damn it!

ILSE. I haven't been home for four days.

MORITZ. — Quiet as a cat!

ILSE. 'Cause I'm wearing my dancing slippers. — My mother's going to faint! — Come up to our house with me!

MORITZ. Where have you been kicking around this time?

ILSE. At the Priapus Club!

MORITZ. The Priapus Club!

ILSE. At Nohl's, at Fehrendorf's, at Padinsky's, at Lenz's, Rank's, Spühler's — all kinds of places! — Ring, ring, ring — she's ready for anything!

MORITZ. Do they paint you?

ILSE. Fehrendorf's painting me as a stylite. I stand on a

Corinthian column. Fehrendorf, I'm telling you, is a first-class crackpot. I squashed one of his tubes last time? He wipes his brush in my hair! I smack him in the ear. He throws his palette at my head. I knock over his easel. He comes after me with his palette knife and we go charging over the sofa and tables and chairs, around and around the studio. There was a sketch behind the stove: Be a good boy, or I'll tear it up! — He promised me amnesty and ended up attacking me — I'm telling you, attacking me — with kisses.

MORITZ. Where do you stay at night when you're in the city?

ILSE. Yesterday I was at Nohl's — day before yesterday at Bojokewitsch's — and Sunday at Oikonomopoulos's. There was champagne at Padinsky's. Valabrégez had just sold his *Plague Victim*. Adolar was drinking out of an ashtray. Lenz was singing "The Babykiller," and Adolar tore the daylights out of his guitar. I was so drunk they had to put me to bed. — — You're still in school, Moritz?

MORITZ. No, no ... I'm leaving this quarter.

ILSE. That's right. Time really flies when you're earning money! — Remember how we used to play robbers? — Wendla Bergmann and you and me and the others, when you'd come out after dinner and have warm goat milk at our house? — What's Wendla doing? I haven't seen her since the flood. — What's Melchi Gabor doing? — Does he still give you those profound looks? — We used to stand across from each other in chorus.

MORITZ. He's a philosopher.

ILSE. Wendla was over at our house not too long ago and gave my mother some jam. I was sitting for Isidor Landauer that day. He needs me for the Virgin Mary with the Christ child. He's disgusting and a jerk. Yikes, like a weathervane! — Do you have a hangover?

MORITZ. From last night! — We put it away like hippopotamuses. I came staggering home at five o'clock.

ILSE. I can tell just by looking at you. — Were there any girls there?

MORITZ. Arabella, a hot little barmaid, an Andalusian! — The owner left us alone with her all night ...

ILSE. I can tell just by looking at you, Moritz! — I don't know what a hangover is. During Carnival last year I went three days and three nights without getting into a bed or out of my clothes. From the ballroom to the café, lunch at the Bella-vista, Tingle-Tangle later on, and the ballroom at night. Lena was with me, and Viola, who's fat. On the third night Heinrich found me.

MORITZ. He was looking for you?

ILSE. He tripped over my arm. I was passed out on a pile of snow. — After that I went over to his place. I didn't leave his apartment for fourteen days — what a ghastly time! — Every morning I had to wrap myself up in his Persian robe and every night I had to walk around the room in a black page-boy costume; white lace cuffs and a white lace collar. Every day he took pictures of me in a different attitude — one time on the back of the sofa as Ariadne, one time as Leda, one time as Ganymede, one time on all fours as a female Nibber-Caneezer. And he was always raving about killing, about shooting, suicide, and gas fumes. First thing in the morning he'd get in bed with a pistol, load it up with bullets, and stick it in my chest: One blink, and I'll pull the trigger! — Oh, he would have done it, Moritz; he would have done it! — Then he'd put the thing in his mouth like a blowpipe. He says it arouses your self-preservatory instincts. And then — *brrrr* — the bullet would have gone straight through my spine.

MORITZ. Is Heinrich still alive?

ILSE. What do I know! — There was a mirror set into the ceiling above the bed. The room was just a closet, but it seemed as tall as a tower and as bright as an opera house. You saw yourself literally hanging in the sky. I had horrible dreams at night. — God, oh God, I couldn't wait for it to get light again! — Good night, Ilse. When you're asleep you look so pretty I could kill you.

MORITZ. Is this Heinrich still alive?

ILSE. I hope not! — One day when he was out buying absinthe I threw his coat on and snuck out in the street. Carnival was over; the police picked me up; what are you doing in a man's clothes? — They took me to headquarters, and Nohl and Fehrendorf and Padinsky and Spühler and Oikonomopoulos, the whole Priapus Club, came and bailed me out. They shipped me to Adolar's studio in a cab. Since then I've been real faithful to the crowd. Fehrendorf's a monkey, Nohl's a pig, Bojokewitsch an owl, Loisson a hyena, Oikonomopoulos a camel — but that's why I love them, every one of them as much as the others, and wouldn't want to be attached to anybody else, even if the world was full of archangels and millionaires!

MORITZ. — I have to go back, Ilse.

ILSE. Come up to our house with me!

MORITZ. — What for? — What for? —

ILSE. To have some warm goat milk! — I've got a curling iron for your hair and I'll hang a little bell around your neck. — We still have a rocking horse you can play with.

MORITZ. I have to go back. — I still have the Sassanids, the Sermon on the Mount, and the parallelepiped on my conscience. — Good night, Ilse!

ILSE. Sweet dreams! ... Do you still go down to the wigwam where Melchi Gabor buried my tomahawk? — Blech! I'll be on the trash heap by the time you guys are ready. *(Ilse hurries away.)*

MORITZ. *(Alone.)* — — — One word is all it would have taken. — *(Calls.)* Ilse! — Ilse! — — She can't hear me, thank God.

— I'm not in the mood. — It takes a clear head and a light heart for that. — What a shame, what a shame to miss the opportunity!

... I'll say I had an enormous crystal mirror over my bed — that I reared a wild filly — that I made her prance around on my carpets in long black silk stockings and black patent leather boots and black long kid gloves and black velvet around her neck — that I smothered her with my pillow in a fit of insanity ... I'll smile when the conversation turns to lust ... I'll — scream! — scream! — to be you, Ilse! — the Priapus Club! — unconsciousness! — it takes my strength away! — this sunny child, this lucky thing — this floozy on my trail of tears! — — oh! — oh! —

— — — — — — —

(In the bushes on the riverbank.) Here I've found it again without looking for it — the grassy bank. The cattails seem to have grown since yesterday. The view through the willows is still the same. — The river's as slow as molten lead. — Before I forget ... *(Moritz takes Mrs. Gabor' s letter out of his pocket and burns it.)* — The sparks are so wild — up and down, this way, that way — souls! — shooting stars! —

Before I started the fire you could still see the grass and a line of light on the horizon. — Now it's gotten dark. Now I won't be going home.

End of Act Two

51

ACT THREE

Scene 1

The conference room. Portraits of Pestalozzi and J. J. Rousseau on the walls. Around a green table lit by several gas lamps sit Professors Schmalz, Blodgett, Starver, Brockenbohn, Fitztongue, and Killaflye. At the head of the table in an elevated armchair is Headmaster Hart-Payne. The custodian, Fetch, cowers by the door.

HART-PAYNE. … Do any of you gentlemen wish to make a further comment? — — Gentlemen! — If we have no choice but to file a motion with the senior undersecretary of education for the expulsion of our delinquent student, then we have no choice for the most compelling reasons. We have no choice so as to atone for the misfortune which has already befallen us, just as we have none so as to render our institution secure against similar catastrophes in the future. We have no choice so as to punish our delinquent student for the demoralizing influence he exerted on his classmates; last of all, we have no choice so as to prevent him from exerting the same influence on his other classmates. We have no choice — and this, gentlemen, may well be the most compelling reason of all, whereby any and all objections will be rendered null and void — namely, that we must protect our institution against the ravages of a suicide epidemic whose outbreak has already occurred at various other institutions and which has hitherto defied all attempts to require students to adhere to the requirement that they exist required by the requirements of their required education. — — Do any of you gentlemen wish to make a further comment?
BLODGETT. I can no longer resist the conclusion that the time has come to open a window somewhere.
FITZTONGUE. Th-th-the current atmosphere r-r-resembles that of a nun-nun-nun-nun-derground catacomb or the archives of th-

th-the Supreme Court building in old Wetzlar described by G-G-G-G-G-Goethe.

HART-PAYNE. Fetch!

FETCH. Yes sir!

HART-PAYNE. Open a window. We have sufficient atmosphere outside, thank God. — Do any of you gentlemen wish to make a further comment?

KILLAFLYE. If my esteemed colleagues wish to have a window opened, I for my part have no objections to raise. I'd only like to request that the window that is wished to be opened not be directly behind my back!

HART-PAYNE. Fetch!

FETCH. Yes sir!

HART-PAYNE. Open the other window. — Do any of you gentlemen wish to make a further comment?

STARVER. Without meaning to prolong the controversy, I for my part would like to call attention to the fact that the other window has been bricked up since last autumn.

HART-PAYNE. Fetch!

FETCH. Yes sir!

HART-PAYNE. Leave the other window closed. — I find myself obliged, gentlemen, to put the motion to a vote. I request that all those colleagues in favor of having the only window which can be opened opened rise from their seats. *(Counts.)* One, two, three. — One, two, three. — Fetch!

FETCH. Yes sir!

HART-PAYNE. Leave the other window closed as well. — I for my part am of the opinion that the atmosphere leaves nothing to be desired! — Do any of you gentlemen wish to make a further comment? — Gentlemen! — Let us assume that we were to neglect to file a motion with the senior undersecretary of education for the expulsion of our delinquent student; in that case the senior undersecretary of education will hold *us* responsible for the misfortune that has befallen us. Of the various other institutions afflicted with the suicide epidemic, those in which more than twenty-five percent have fallen victim to its ravages have been suspended by the senior undersecretary of education. To protect our institution against this most shattering blow is our duty as guardians and keepers of our institution. It hurts us deeply, my esteemed colleagues, that we are not in a position to admit the auxiliary qualifications of our delinquent student as mitigating circumstances. Lenient treatment, which could be justified with respect to our delinquent student, could *not* be justified with respect to the acutely threatened existence of our institution. We find ourselves under the necessity of condemning the guilty lest we ourselves, the innocent, be condemned. — Fetch!

FETCH. Yes sir!

HART-PAYNE. Bring him up. *(Fetch exits.)*

FITZTONGUE. If th-th-th-the current atmosphere is officially viewed as leaving little or nothing to be desired, then I should like to make a motion that during summer vacation the other window be br-br-br-br-br-bricked up as well!

KILLAFLYE. If our room strikes our dear esteemed colleague Fitztongue as insufficiently ventilated, then I should like to make a motion that our esteemed colleague Fitztongue have a ventilator installed in his upper sinuses.

FITZTONGUE. Uh-uh-uh-I don't have to stand for this! — Uh-uh-uh — I don't have to stand for his rudeness! — I'm in possession of all f-f-f-five of my senses…!

HART-PAYNE. I must request that our colleagues Killaflye and Fitztongue show a measure of decorum. Our delinquent student would appear to be on the stairway already. *(Fetch opens the door, and Melchior, pale but composed, steps before the assembly.)* Step up to the table! — After Mr. Stiefel received word of the wicked crime his son had committed, the distraught father, in the hope of thereby possibly garnering clues as to the cause of the abominable misdeed, searched the effects left behind by his son Moritz and thereby chanced to find, in a place irrelevant to the discussion, a document which, while not in and of itself capable of rendering the abominable misdeed comprehensible, does provide us with an unfortunately all too adequate explanation of the criminal's moral derangement in the period immediately preceding the crime. Written in dialogue form, entitled "Copulation," furnished with life-sized illustrations, bursting with the most shameless obscenities, the twenty-page treatise in question could satisfy the most sophisticated demands a depraved libertine could make upon pornographic literature. —

MELCHIOR. I …

HART-PAYNE. You are to remain silent! — After Mr. Stiefel had furnished us with the document in question and we had given the distraught father a promise at all costs to identify its author, the handwriting at hand was compared with the handwriting of every fellow student of the deceased transgressor and revealed, in the unanimous judgment of the entire faculty, and in complete accord with the expert opinion of our highly regarded colleague the professor of calligraphy, the most serious imaginable similarity with *yours.* —

MELCHIOR. I …

HART-PAYNE. You are to remain silent! — Notwithstanding the overwhelming fact of similarity, as adduced to by unimpeachable authorities, we believe that we may be permitted to refrain for the time being from taking any further steps, in order that we may interrogate the delinquent student concerning the crime against decency with which he is charged, in connection with the motive for suicide which resulted therefrom. —

MELCHIOR. I …

HART-PAYNE. You are to answer the precisely formulated questions that I shall put to you in order, one after the other, with a simple and respectful yes or no. — Fetch!

FETCH. Yes sir!

HART-PAYNE. The file! — — I shall request that from this point onward our secretary, Professor Killaflye, take minutes that correspond as strictly as possible to the spoken proceedings. — *(To Melchior.)* Are you familiar with this document?

MELCHIOR. Yes.

HART-PAYNE. Are you familiar with the content of this document?

MELCHIOR. Yes.

HART-PAYNE. Is the handwriting in this document your own?

MELCHIOR. Yes.

HART-PAYNE. Are you responsible for the composition of this obscene document?

MELCHIOR. Yes. — Sir, I wish you'd show me *one* obscenity in it.

HART-PAYNE. You are to answer the precisely formulated questions that I shall put to you with a simple and respectful yes or no!

MELCHIOR. What I wrote is nothing more and nothing less than a fact well known to you!

HART-PAYNE. This scoundrel!

MELCHIOR. I wish you'd show me one offense against decency in what I wrote!

HART-PAYNE. Do you actually think I mean to sit here and play the fool for you?! — Fetch!

MELCHIOR. I ...

HART-PAYNE. You have as little respect for the dignity of your assembled teachers as you have a sense of decency regarding the deeply rooted human feeling for the discretion of the modesty of a moral order! — Fetch!

FETCH. Yes sir!

HART-PAYNE. This is Langenscheidt's three-hour course in agglutinative Volapük!

MELCHIOR. I ...

HART-PAYNE. I shall request that our secretary, Professor Killaflye, close the minutes!

MELCHIOR. I'm ...

HART-PAYNE. You are to remain silent! — Fetch!

FETCH. Yes sir!

HART-PAYNE. Take him down.

Scene 2

Cemetery in pouring rain. His raised umbrella in his hand, Reverend Bleekhead is standing in front of an open grave. To his right, Mr. Stiefel, his friend Ziegenmelker, and Uncle Probst. On the left, Headmaster Hart-Payne with Professor Brockenbohn. Boys from the school complete the circle. At some distance, by a badly weathered gravestone, Martha and Ilse.

REVEREND BLEEKHEAD. ... For whosoever spurns the grace which the eternal Father has bestown upon those born in sin, he shall die a *spiritual* death! — But whosoever has lived in evil and served evil in willful carnal denial of the honor due unto God, he shall die a *corporeal* death! — Yet whosoever has wickedly cast off the cross which the all-merciful One has inflicted upon him for his sins, truly, truly, I say to you, he shall die an *eternal* death! — *(Throws a shovel of dirt into the grave.)* — Let us, however, who continue and continue to tread the path of thorns, praise the Lord, the Almighty, and give thanks unto Him for the mysteries of His merciful grace. For as truly as *this* soul died a *threefold* death, so truly will the Lord God lead the righteous to salvation and eternal life. — Amen.

MR. STIEFEL. *(Choking back tears, throws a shovel of dirt into the grave.)* The boy was no son of mine! — The boy was no son of mine! — Even when he was little I didn't like him!

HART-PAYNE. *(Throws a shovel of dirt into the grave.)* Suicide as the most serious imaginable offense against the moral order constitutes the most serious proof imaginable of the moral order, in that the perpetrator spares the moral order the necessity of pronouncing its verdict and thus confirms its existence.

PROFESSOR BROCKENBOHN. *(Throws a shovel of dirt into the grave.)* Despicable — debauched — degenerate — depraved — and dissolute!

UNCLE PROBST. *(Throws a shovel of dirt into the grave.)* I wouldn't have believed my own mother if she'd told me a child could treat his parents so rottenly.

FRIEND ZIEGENMELKER. *(Throws a shovel of dirt into the grave.)* To do a thing like that to a father who day and night for twenty years has thought of nothing but the welfare of his child!

REVEREND BLEEKHEAD. *(Pressing Mr. Stiefel's hand.)* We know that for those who love God all things work together for the best. (I Corinthians 12:15) — Bethink yourself of the disconsolate mother and endeavor to replace with redoubled love what she has lost!

HART-PAYNE. *(Pressing Mr. Stiefel's hand.)* It's quite probable he would not have passed in any case!

PROFESSOR BROCKENBOHN. *(Pressing Mr. Stiefel's hand.)* And if he had passed, we most positively would have held him back next spring!

UNCLE PROBST. *(Pressing Mr. Stiefel's hand.)* Your very first obligation now is to yourself! You're the head of a family…!

FRIEND ZIEGENMELKER. *(Pressing Mr. Stiefel's hand.)* You leave it all to me! — Nasty, nasty bit of weather; makes my guts jump. — If you don't intervene immediately with a couple of stiff grogs, you can kiss your heart valves goodbye!

MR. STIEFEL. *(Blowing his nose.)* The boy was no son of mine … the boy was no son of mine … *(Mr. Stiefel, led by Reverend Bleekhead, Headmaster Hart-Payne, Professor Brockenbohn, Uncle Probst, and Ziegenmelker, exits. — The rain lets up.)*

HANSY. *(Throws a shovel of dirt into the grave.)* Rest in peace, old sport! — Give my regards to my eternal brides, their sacrifice is not forgotten, and commend me most devotedly to our gracious Lord — you poor stooge! — For the sake of your angelic innocence they'll put a scarecrow on your grave …

GEORGE. Any sign of the gun?

ROBERT. They don't have to look for any gun!

ERNST. Did you see him, Robert?

ROBERT. A goddamned filthy slimy fraud! — Who saw him? — Who?!

OTTO. That's the thing! — They'd put a sheet over him.

GEORGE. Was his tongue hanging out?

ROBERT. His eyes! — That's why they'd put the sheet on.

OTTO. Horrible!

HANSY. Are you quite sure he hanged himself?

ERNST. They say there was nothing left of his head.

OTTO. Nonsense! — Ridiculous!

ROBERT. I had the rope in my hand! — I've never seen somebody who hanged himself that they didn't cover up.

GEORGE. He couldn't have found a ruder way to send his regards!

HANSY. What the hell, they say hanging's very pretty.

OTTO. The thing is, he still owes me five marks. We had a bet. He swore he wouldn't flunk.

HANSY. It's your fault he's lying here. You called him a show-off.

OTTO. Hoop-de-doo, I have to cram all night myself. If he'd learned his Greek literature he wouldn't have needed to hang himself!

ERNST. Have you done the essay, Otto?

OTTO. Just the first paragraph.

ERNST. I have no idea what I'm going to write.

GEORGE. Weren't you there when Schmalz assigned it?

HANSY. I'm going to cobble together something from Democritus.

ERNST. I'll see if I can find anything in *Meyer's Abridged*.

OTTO. Have you done the Virgil for tomorrow? — — — — —

(The boys exit. — Martha and Ilse approach the grave.)

ILSE. Hurry, hurry! — The gravediggers are coming.

MARTHA. Shouldn't we maybe wait, Ilse?

ILSE. What for? — We'll bring some new ones. We'll keep bringing them! — There's plenty more where these came from.

MARTHA. You're right, Ilse! — *(She throws a wreath of ivy on the grave. Ilse opens her apron and lets a stream of fresh anemones rain down on the coffin.)* I'll dig up our roses. I get beaten anyway! — They'll really thrive here.

ILSE. I'll water them every time I go by. I'll bring over forget-me-nots from the meadow and irises from home.

MARTHA. It should be spectacular! Spectacular!

ILSE. I was already across the bridge when I heard the bang.

MARTHA. Poor thing!

ILSE. And I know the reason, too, Martha.

MARTHA. Did he say something to you?

ILSE. Parallelepiped! But don't tell anybody.

MARTHA. Cross my heart.

ILSE. — Here's the gun.

MARTHA. That's why they couldn't find it!

ILSE. I took it right out of his hand when I came by in the morning.

MARTHA. Give it to me, Ilse! — Please give it to me!

ILSE. No, I'm saving it as a souvenir.

MARTHA. Is it true, Ilse, that he's lying in there without a head?

ILSE. He must have loaded it with water! — There was blood spattered all over the cattails. His brains were hanging in the willows.

Scene 3

Mr. and Mrs. Gabor.

MRS. GABOR. ... They needed a scapegoat. The accusations were getting louder and they couldn't just let the matter rest. And now my child has had the bad luck to run afoul of those pedants at precisely the wrong time, and you expect me, his own mother, to help his executioners finish their work? — God forbid!

MR. GABOR. — For fourteen years I've observed your imaginative educational methods and said nothing. They were at odds with my own ideas. It has always been my conviction that a child is not a plaything; that a child is entitled to our utmost seriousness. But I told myself, if one person's charm and intellect are capable of replacing another's earnest principles, then they might be preferable to the earnest principles. — I'm not reproaching you, Fanny. But don't stand in my way when I try to atone for the injustice you and I have done the boy!

MRS. GABOR. I'll stand in your way so long as there's a drop of warm blood in me! My child would be lost in the reformatory. Maybe a criminal mind can be improved in an institution like that. I don't know. But a good-natured person will turn into a criminal there as surely as a plant will die if you deprive it of air and sunlight. I'm not aware of any injustice on my part. I continue to thank heaven for having shown me the way to awaken an upright character and a noble mind in my child. What has he done that's so terrible? It would never occur to me to make excuses for him — it's not his fault he was expelled from school. And if it were his fault, he's certainly paid for it. You may understand all this better. You may theoretically be completely in the right. But I cannot allow my only child to be stripped from me and hounded to his death!

MR. GABOR. That's out of our hands, Fanny. — That's a risk we accepted along with our happiness. Those too weak to march must fall by the wayside. And ultimately it isn't the worst thing that could happen if the inevitable occurs ahead of time. May Heaven spare us that! Our task is to steady the weak of will to the best of our knowledge and abilities. — It wasn't his fault he was expelled from school. Nor would it have been his fault if he *hadn't* been expelled from school! — You're too optimistic. You see a cocky little prank when what we're dealing with is a deeply flawed personality. You women aren't competent to judge such things. The person who can write the kind of thing that Melchior wrote must be tainted in the very core of his being. The marrow is affected. A halfway healthy personality couldn't bring himself to do a thing like that. None of us is a saint; every one of us veers from the straight and narrow. What he wrote, however, represents a *principle*. What he wrote bears no resemblance to a momentary accidental lapse; it documents with horrifying clarity an outspoken *intention,* that natural proclivity, that penchant for *immorality* for the sake of immorality. What he wrote manifests that exceptional spiritual corruption we lawyers characterize with the expression "*moral insanity.*" — Whether anything can be done about his condition, I am not in a position to say. If we wish to preserve one glimmer of hope and, most important, to preserve our spotless consciences as the parents of the individual, it is time for us to go to work with firmness and in all seriousness.

— Let's not argue anymore, Fanny! I can feel how hard it will be for you. I know you adore him because he mirrors so completely your natural virtuosity. Rise above yourself! Now is the time to finally be selfless toward your son!

MRS. GABOR. God help me, there's no fighting an attitude like this! — Only a *man* could talk this way. Only a *man* can let himself be so blinded by the dead letter. Only a *man* can so blindly ignore what's staring him in the face! — I have treated Melchior responsibly and prudently since the very first day I saw he was sensitive to impressions from his environment. But are we responsible for *accidents?* You could get hit in the head with a falling brick tomorrow morning, and then your best friend comes along — your father comes along, and instead of taking care of your injuries he steps on you! — I refuse to stand and watch while my son gets slaughtered. That's what a mother is for. — It's absurd! It's unbelievable. What in the world did he write, anyway? Could you ask for more convincing proof of his harmlessness, of his stupidity, of his childish innocence, than the fact that he could write a thing like that! — You'd have to have no conception of human nature — you'd have to be a totally soulless bureaucrat or hopelessly narrowminded to see a sign of moral corruption in this! — — Say whatever you want. If you put Melchior in the reformatory, I'm divorcing you! And then I'll see if I can't somewhere in the world find the resources to save my child from destruction.

MR. GABOR. You're going to have to reconcile yourself to it — if not today, then tomorrow. It isn't easy for anyone to come to terms with misfortune. I'll stand by your side, and when your courage threatens to waver I'll spare no pains and no sacrifice to lighten your heart. The future looks so gray to me, so clouded — all I'd need now would be to lose you, too.

MRS. GABOR. I won't see him again; I won't see him again. He can't stand vulgarity. He'll never adjust to the filth. He'll lose all restraint; he's haunted by the most ghastly example! — And if I see him again — God, God, that springlike joy in his heart — that sunny laughter of his — everything, everything — that childish determination to fight for goodness and justice — oh, that bright clear morning sky I nurtured in his soul as my highest good … Take *me,* if the injustice cries out for retribution! Take me! Do whatever you want with me! *I'm* the one to blame. — But keep your frightful hands off my child.

61

MR. GABOR. He has committed an offense!

MRS. GABOR. *He has not committed an offense!*

MR. GABOR. He has committed an offense! — — — I would have given anything to be able to spare you in your boundless love. — This morning a woman came to me, beside herself, hardly able to speak, with *this* letter in her hand — a letter to her fifteen-year-old daughter. She'd opened it out of stupid curiosity; the girl wasn't home. — In the letter, Melchior tells this fifteen-year-old child that what he did is leaving him no peace, that he has sinned against her, et cetera, et cetera, but will of course take full responsibility for everything. She shouldn't fret, even if she thinks there might have been consequences, he's already taking steps to find help; his expulsion makes this easier for him; what started as a mistake may yet lead to their happiness — and more absurd twaddle of the same sort.

MRS. GABOR. Impossible!

MR. GABOR. The letter is forged. A case of fraud. An attempt to exploit the widely known fact of his expulsion. I haven't spoken to the boy as of yet — but look at the handwriting! Look at the style!

MRS. GABOR. A filthy, shameless outrage!

MR. GABOR. I'm afraid so!

MRS. GABOR. No, no — never, never!

MR. GABOR. It will be all the better for us. — The woman wrung her hands and asked me what she should do. I told her she shouldn't let her fifteen-year-old daughter climb around in haylofts. Fortunately she left the letter here with me. — If we send Melchior to a different school now, where he wouldn't even be under parental supervision, in three weeks we'll be facing the identical situation — another expulsion — his springlike heart is developing a taste for it. — Tell me, Fanny, what am I supposed to do with the boy?!

MRS. GABOR. — The reformatory —

MR. GABOR. The...?

MRS. GABOR. ... Reformatory!

MR. GABOR. What he will find there above all is what was wrongly withheld from him at home: iron discipline, earnest principles, and moral constraints to which he must submit without exception. — Beyond that, the reformatory is not the chamber of horrors you imagine it to be. The institution stresses the development of a Christian way of thinking and feeling. A boy finally learns there to want what is *good,* rather than what is *entertaining,*

and in all his dealings to consider not his personality, but the *law*.
— — Half an hour ago I received a telegram from my brother confirming the woman's statements. Melchior confided in him and asked him for two hundred marks to run away to England …
MRS. GABOR. *(Covers her face.)* Merciful heaven!

Scene 4

The reformatory. — A corridor. — Diethelm, Reinhold, Rupert, Helmuth, Gaston, and Melchior.

DIETHELM. Here's a quarter-mark piece!
REINHOLD. So?
DIETHELM. So I put it on the floor and we all stand around it. Whoever hits it can have it.
RUPERT. You in, Melchior?
MELCHIOR. No, thank you.
HELMUTH. The little Joseph!
GASTON. He's worn out. He's here to recover.
MELCHIOR. *(Aside.)* It isn't smart of me to stay apart from them. Everybody's watching me. I have to participate — otherwise I'm sunk. — — Captivity makes them suicidal. — — If I break my neck, it's OK! If I make it out, it's also OK! I can't lose. — I'm getting to be friends with Rupert, he knows his way around here. — I'll give him a Bible lesson, tell him about Moab, and Lot and his daughters, and Judah's daughter-in-law Tamar, and Queen Vashti and Abishag the Shunammite. — He's got the most afflicted physiognomy of anybody in our sector.
RUPERT. Got it!
HELMUTH. I'm coming!
GASTON. Day after tomorrow, maybe!
HELMUTH. Right now! — Now! — Oh God, oh God …
ALL. *Summa — summa cum laude!*
RUPERT. *(Taking the coin.)* Thanks very much!
HELMUTH. Give it here, you bastard!
RUPERT. Pigface!

HELMUTH. Derelict!

RUPERT. *(Hits him in the face.)* Here! *(Runs away.)*

HELMUTH. *(Chasing him.)* I'll beat the shit out of him!

THE OTHERS. *(Running after them.)* Sic 'em, boys! Charge! Charge! Charge! Charge!

MELCHIOR. *(Alone, facing the window.)* — That's where the lightning conductor comes down. — You have to wrap a handkerchief around it. — Whenever I think about her, the blood rushes to my head. And Moritz is like lead in my feet. — — I'll go to the editor. Pay me by the hundred lines; I'll be a hawker in the street! — Be a stringer — write — local news — ethics — psychophysics … it's not so easy to starve anymore. Soup kitchens, temperance halls. — The building's sixty feet tall and the stucco is crumbling off … She hates me — she hates me because I stole her freedom. No matter what I do, it's still rape. — I can only hope that gradually, as the years go by … In eight days there's a new moon. Tomorrow I'll oil the hinges. By Saturday, no matter what, I have to know who has the key. — At the Sunday night service a cataleptic seizure — God willing, no one else will be sick! — I can see it all as clearly as if it had already happened. I can get over the sill without any trouble — one swing — one handhold — but you have to wrap a handkerchief around it. — — Here comes the Grand Inquisitor. *(Melchior exits left. Dr. Procrustes enters, right, with a locksmith.)*

DR. PROCRUSTES. … Granted, these windows are on the fourth floor and we've planted stinging nettles underneath them. But what do these degenerates care about stinging nettles? — Last winter one of them climbed out a skylight, and we had all the fuss of retrieval, and transport, and burial …

THE LOCKSMITH. You want me to make the grating out of wrought iron?

DR. PROCRUSTES. Wrought iron, yes — and since it can't be set into the wall, use rivets.

Scene 5

A bedroom. — Mrs. Bergmann, Ina Müller, and Dr. Seltzer, the public health officer. — Wendla in bed.

DR. SELTZER. How old are you?

WENDLA. Fourteen and a half.

DR. SELTZER. I've been prescribing Blaud's Pills for fifteen years now and have obtained the most dazzling results in a great number of cases. I find them preferable to cod-liver oil and iron tonics. Begin by taking three to four pills a day and increase the dosage as rapidly as you can tolerate. I directed the young baroness Elfriede von Witzleben to increase her dosage by one pill every three days. The baroness misunderstood me and increased it by three pills every one day. After little more than three weeks, the baroness was able to accompany her mama to the spa in Bad Pyrmont for a post-therapeutic cure. — I shall excuse you from tiring walks and extra meals. In exchange, my dear child, you must promise me that, as soon as your appetites have returned, you will exercise vigorously and not be ashamed to ask for nourishment. At that point the palpitations will quickly subside — and the headaches, the chills, the dizziness — and our terrible indigestion. Only eight days after beginning her cure, the young baroness Elfriede von Witzleben was having an entire roast chicken with new potatoes in their skins for breakfast.

MRS. BERGMANN. Can I offer you a glass of wine, Doctor?

DR. SELTZER. Thank you, my dear Mrs. Bergmann. My conveyance is waiting. Don't let it upset you so much. In a few weeks our dear little patient will be as fresh and lively as a gazelle again. Rest assured. — Goodbye, Mrs. Bergmann. Goodbye, dear child. Goodbye, ladies. Goodbye. *(Mrs. Bergmann leaves the room with him.)*

INA. *(At the window.)* — The leaves on your plane tree are turning already. — Can you see it from bed? — Short-lived splendor, hardly even worth the joy of seeing it come and go like this. — I have to leave soon myself. Müller's meeting me in front of the post office and I have to go to the dressmaker's first. Mucki's getting his first little pair of pants, and I told Karl he'd get a new woolen suit for the winter.

WENDLA. Sometimes I'll feel so wonderful — everything sunshine and happiness. I wouldn't have thought it was possible to feel so good! I'll feel like going outside, out on the grass in the evening sun, and looking for primroses along the river, and sitting on the riverbank and dreaming ... And then this *toothache* starts, and I think I'm going to die before the sun goes down tomorrow; I feel hot and cold, everything starts going dark, and then the monster comes fluttering in — —

— Every time I wake up, I see Mother crying. Oh, that hurts me so much — I can't tell you, Ina!

INA. — Can I prop up your pillow for you?

MRS. BERGMANN. *(Returning.)* He thinks the vomiting will stop; and then it will be safe for you to get up again ... I also think it's better if you get up soon, Wendla.

INA. The next time I drop in, maybe you'll be running around the house again. — Take care, Mother. I absolutely must get to the dressmaker's. God bless you, Wendla dear. *(Kisses her.)* Get well very, very soon now!

WENDLA. Goodbye, Ina. — Bring me some primroses next time you come. Goodbye. Say hello to the boys for me. *(Ina exits.)* What else did he say out there, Mother?

MRS. BERGMANN. He didn't say anything. — He said Miss von Witzleben also had a tendency to faint. That's almost always the way it is with anemia.

WENDLA. Did he say I have anemia, Mother?

MRS. BERGMANN. He said you should have lots of milk and meat and vegetables when your appetite comes back.

WENDLA. Oh, Mother, Mother, I don't think I have anemia.

MRS. BERGMANN. You have anemia, baby. There's nothing to worry about, Wendla, nothing to worry about; you have anemia.

WENDLA. No, Mother, no! I know it. I feel it. I don't have anemia. I have dropsy ...

MRS. BERGMANN. You have anemia. Didn't he just say you had anemia? Stop worrying about it, darling. It will get better.

WENDLA. It won't get better. I have dropsy. I'm going to die, Mother. — Oh, Mother, I'm going to die!

MRS. BERGMANN. Baby, you aren't going to die! You aren't going to die ... Merciful heavens, you aren't going to die!

WENDLA. Then what are you crying so miserably for?

MRS. BERGMANN. You aren't going to die — baby! You don't have dropsy. My little girl, you have a *baby!* You have a baby! — Oh, why did you do this to me!

WENDLA. — I didn't do anything to you —

MRS. BERGMANN. Oh, stop denying it, Wendla! — I know everything. I couldn't bring myself to say anything before. — Wendla, my Wendla…!

WENDLA. But that's not possible, Mother. I'm not married…!

MRS. BERGMANN. Great God Almighty — that's just it, you're not married! That's the terrible thing! — Wendla, Wendla, Wendla, what have you done!

WENDLA. I honestly don't remember anymore! We were lying in the hay … I never loved anybody in the world except you, you, Mother.

MRS. BERGMANN. Sweetheart —

WENDLA. Oh, Mother, why didn't you tell me everything!

MRS. BERGMANN. Baby, baby, let's not make it any harder for each other! Pull yourself together! Don't despair, my baby! Tell that to a fourteen-year-old girl? Goodness, I'd sooner have watched the sun go out. I didn't treat you any different than my dear, kind mother treated me. — Oh, let's trust in the Lord, Wendla; let's do our part and hope for mercy! You see, baby, nothing has happened *yet.* And as long as we don't lose courage ourselves, the Lord won't forsake us either. — Be *brave,* Wendla, be *brave!* — Tsk. You're sitting at the window and you let your hands rest in your lap because everything is turning out for the best after all, and then it all caves in so suddenly that your heart feels like breaking right then and there … Wh — Why are you shaking?

WENDLA. Somebody knocked on the door.

MRS. BERGMANN. I didn't hear anything, sweetie. — *(Goes to the door and opens it.)*

WENDLA. Oh! I heard it very clearly. — — Who's out there?

MRS. BERGMANN. — No one — — Old Mrs. Schmidt from Garden Street. — — — You came at just the right time, Mother Schmidt.

Scene 6

Men and women working in a vineyard on a hillside. — In the west the sun is setting behind mountain peaks. From the valley, the clear sound of bells. On the highest terrace of vines, beneath the overhanging cliffs, Hansy Rilow and Ernst Röbel are rolling in the dying grass.

ERNST. I worked too hard.

HANSY. Let's not be sad! — Life's too short.

ERNST. You see them hanging there but you're worn out — and tomorrow they'll be crushed.

HANSY. Being tired's as unbearable as being hungry.

ERNST. Oh, I am worn out.

HANSY. This one last glowing muscatel!

ERNST. I can't summon the strength for it.

HANSY. If I pull the branch down it will bob around above our mouths. Neither of us has to move. We'll bite the fruit off and let the bare stems snap back up to the vine.

ERNST. No sooner have you made your decision when, lo and behold, your vanished strength comes surging up again.

HANSY. And the flaming firmament — and the evening bells — It's never going to get much better than this.

ERNST. — Sometimes I can already see myself as Reverend Röbel — an affectionate little housewife, an extensive library, rights and privileges in every circle of society. You get six days to think, and on the seventh day you open your mouth. When you go out for a walk, schoolboys and schoolgirls shake hands with you, and when you come home the coffee is steaming, the cake is on the table, and girls are bringing in apples through the garden gate. — Can you imagine anything nicer?

HANSY. I imagine half-closed eyelashes, half-open lips, and Turkish draperies. — I don't believe in grand emotions. Look, the reason our parents wear long faces is to cover up their stupid thoughts. When they're by themselves they call each other block-heads just like we do. I know they do. — When I'm a millionaire,

I'll build a monument to God. — Think of the future as a bowl of fresh milk with sugar and cinnamon. One man spills it and cries, the other one churns it and sweats. Why not skim the cream off? — Or don't you think we could learn how?

ERNST. — We'll skim the cream off!

HANSY. And let the chickens eat the rest. — I've slipped out of plenty of nooses already ...

ERNST. We'll skim the cream off, Hansy! — Why are you laughing?

HANSY. Are you at it again already?

ERNST. One of us has to start.

HANSY. Maybe, when we look back on an afternoon like this thirty years from now, it will seem indescribably nice!

ERNST. And now it's happening without any effort at all.

HANSY. Why shouldn't it?

ERNST. If a person happened to be by himself — he might even cry.

HANSY. Let's not be sad! — *(Kisses him on the mouth.)*

ERNST. *(Kissing him.)* When I left the house I was thinking I'd only talk to you and then go right back.

HANSY. I was expecting you. — Virtue's not a bad thing to wear, but it's cut for a big man.

ERNST. We're still tripping on the cuffs. — I never would have calmed down if I hadn't run into you. — I love you, Hansy, like I've never loved another soul ...

HANSY. Let's not be sad! — Maybe when we look back on an afternoon like this thirty years from now it will seem ridiculous! — And now it's all so nice! The mountains are glowing; the grapes are hanging in our mouths, and the evening wind is stroking the cliffs like a little teasing kitten ...

Scene 7

*A clear November night. Withered leaves rustle on the trees
and bushes. Tattered clouds are racing beneath the moon.
Melchior climbs over the cemetery wall.*

MELCHIOR. *(Jumping down inside the wall.)* The pack won't follow me in here. — While they're combing through the brothels, I
can catch my breath and see where I stand ... My coat torn to
pieces, my pockets empty — the most harmless person could do
whatever he wanted to me. — During the day I'll have to try to
keep going in the woods. I knocked over a cross. — The flowers
didn't freeze until today! — The ground is barren all around ... In
the land of the dead! — Climbing out of that skylight wasn't as
hard as walking through here! — This is the one thing I wasn't prepared for ... I'm hanging over the abyss — everything has fallen
away around me, vanished — Oh, I wish I'd stayed there! Why her
and not me! — Why not the one who's guilty! — The mysteries of
providence! — I would have broken rocks and gone hungry...!
What keeps me on my feet? — One crime leads to another. I've
been relegated to the swamp. Not enough strength to put an end
to it ... I wasn't bad! — I wasn't bad! — I wasn't bad ... No mor-
tal has ever walked on graves so enviously. — Pah — I wouldn't
have the courage! — Oh, if I could just go crazy — this very night!
I have to look over there where the recent ones are! — The wind
whistles in a different key on every gravestone — a stifling sym-
phony! — The rotten wreaths are torn to pieces, they dangle on
their long ribbons in clumps around the marble crosses — a forest
of scarecrows! — Scarecrows on every grave, each more ghastly
than the others — high as houses, and the devils run for their lives.
— The gold lettering has a cold gleam ... The weeping willow
moans and trails its giant fingers over the inscription ...
     A praying cherub — A tablet —
     A cloud is throwing its shadow down here. — The way it rushes
and howls! — as if an army marching in the east is driving it higher
and higher. — Not a star in the sky —

A plot with holly around it? — Holly? — — Little girl! ...

And I murdered her. — I murdered her! — I have nothing left except despair. — I can't cry here. — Out of here! — Out!

MORITZ. *(His head under his arm, he comes plodding over the graves.)* Just a minute, Melchior! This is a rare opportunity. You have no idea how crucial the timing and the location are ...

MELCHIOR. Where did you come from?!

MORITZ. From over there. You knocked over my cross. I'm by the wall. — Give me your hand, Melchior...!

MELCHIOR. You are *not* Moritz Stiefel!

MORITZ. Give me your hand. I'm quite sure you'll be grateful. It will never be this easy again! We're meeting by a rare and happy chance. — I came up 'specially ...

MELCHIOR. You mean you don't sleep?

MORITZ. Not what you call sleeping. — We sit on church steeples, on gables — wherever we want ...

MELCHIOR. In torment?

MORITZ. For the fun of it. — We skim past maypoles, past lonely forest chapels. We hover over the scenes of accidents, over public meetings, fairgrounds, parks. — When we're inside people's houses we crouch in chimneys and behind the bed-curtains. — Give me your hand. — We don't fraternize with each other, but we see and hear everything that's going on in the world. We know that everything people do and strive for is stupid, and we laugh at it.

MELCHIOR. What good does that do?

MORITZ. What does it need to do any good for? — We're no longer reachable for anything, neither good nor evil. We stand high, high above terrestrial concerns — each one of us for himself alone. We don't fraternize with each other, because it's too boring for us. None of us has anything left to lose. In our infinite sublimity, we are as far from sorrow as from rejoicing. We're satisfied with ourselves, and that's what counts! — We view the living with unspeakable contempt, to the point where we hardly even pity them. They amuse us with their little activities, because there really isn't anything to be pitied about a person who's still alive. We smile at their tragedies — each of us for himself — and make our own observations about them. — Give me your hand! When you give me your hand you'll fall over laughing at the feelings you're having as you give me your hand ...

MELCHIOR. Doesn't that disgust you?

MORITZ. We're too sublime for that. We smile! — I was standing among the mourners at my funeral. It was a first-rate entertainment for me. That's what sublimity is, Melchior! I wailed and wailed and then sneaked over to the wall to laugh until I ached. Our incomparable sublimity is truly the only point of view that makes all the garbage digestible ... I'll bet they were even laughing at *me,* before I made the leap.

MELCHIOR. — I'm not interested in laughing at myself.

MORITZ. ... The living are truly not to be pitied for being alive! — I admit I never would have guessed it, either. And now it's incomprehensible to me how anyone can be so naive. Now I can see through the fraud so clearly there's not a wisp of fog left. — How can you even hesitate, Melchior! Give me your hand! In the snap of a neck you'll be sky-high above yourself. — Your life is a sin of omission ...

MELCHIOR. — Can you forget?

MORITZ. We can do anything. Give me your hand! We can feel sorry for youth, the way it takes its timidness for idealism, and for old age, the way its heart breaks with stoic superiority. We see emperors trembling over popular songs, and street shysters shaking at the sound of the last trumpet. We ignore the comedian's mask and see the poet putting his mask on in the dark. We behold the contented man in his impoverishment, and in the man who "labors and is heavy laden" we see the capitalist. We observe people in love and see them blush at each other, suspecting that they're deceived deceivers. We see parents bringing children into the world in order to be able to say to them: How lucky you are to have parents like us! — and see the children going out and doing the same thing. We can eavesdrop on innocence in its lonely extremities of love, and on the two-bit whore reading Schiller ... We see God and the devil making fools of each other, and we nurture in ourselves the absolutely unshakable conviction that both of them are drunk ... A peace of mind, a contentedness, Melchior — ! You only have to give me your pinkie. — You might be an old, old man before you have another opportunity like this!

MELCHIOR. — If I accept, Moritz, and we seal it with a handshake, I'll be doing it out of self-contempt. — I'm an outcast now. What gave me courage is buried in the ground. I no longer consider myself worthy of noble impulses — and I see nothing, nothing left that could stand between me and my destruction. — I feel like the most loathsome creature in the universe ...

MORITZ. Why are you hesitating? *(A masked man enters.)*

THE MASKED MAN. *(To Melchior.)* You're shaking with hunger. You're in no condition to judge. — *(To Moritz.)* Leave.

MELCHIOR. Who are you?

THE MASKED MAN. That will become clear. — *(To Moritz.)* Get out of here! — What business do you have here! — Why aren't you wearing your head?

MORITZ. I shot myself.

THE MASKED MAN. Then stay where you belong, you're finished! Don't pester us here with your grave smells. It's unbelievable — take a look at your fingers. Feh! It's starting to crumble.

MORITZ. Please don't send me away ...

MELCHIOR. Sir, who are you?

MORITZ. Don't send me away! Please! Let me be a part of things for a little while longer; I won't disagree with you about *anything.* — — It's so horrid down there.

THE MASKED MAN. Then why do you go on and on about your *sublimity?!* — You know it's all humbug — sour grapes! Why do you deliberately *lie,* you — bogy! — If it means so much to you, I don't care if you stick around. But be careful with the mumbo jumbo, my friend — and do me a favor and leave your rotting hand out of this!

MELCHIOR. Are you or aren't you going to tell me who you are?

THE MASKED MAN. No. — I suggest that you trust me. To begin with, I'd make sure you get out of here.

MELCHIOR. You're — my father?!

THE MASKED MAN. Wouldn't you recognize your dear father by his voice?

MELCHIOR. No.

THE MASKED MAN. Your dear father is, as we speak, seeking comfort in the strong arms of your mother. — I'll open up the world for you. This temporary distress of yours is due to your miserable situation. It will seem ridiculous as soon as you've got a warm dinner under your belt.

MELCHIOR. *(To himself.)* Only one of them can be the devil! — *(Aloud.)* With all the things I'm guilty of, a hot dinner isn't going to give me back my peace of mind!

THE MASKED MAN. That depends on the dinner! — I can tell you this much: The little girl would have given birth exquisitely. She was ideally built. It was the abortion methods of Mother

Schmidt that killed her. — — I'll introduce you to people. I'll give you the opportunity to broaden your horizons in the most fabulous way. You won't miss a single interesting thing the world has to offer.

MELCHIOR. Who are you? Who are you? — I can't put myself in the hands of somebody I don't know.

THE MASKED MAN. You won't get to know me unless you put yourself in my hands.

MELCHIOR. You think so?

THE MASKED MAN. It's a fact! — And by the way, you don't have any choice.

MELCHIOR. I can give my hand to my friend whenever I want to.

THE MASKED MAN. Your friend is a charlatan. Nobody smiles if they've got a penny left in cash. The sublime humorist is the most woeful, pitiable creature in creation!

MELCHIOR. Be that as it may; if you don't tell me who you are, I'm going to give the humorist my hand!

THE MASKED MAN. — Well?!

MORITZ. He's right, Melchior. I was exaggerating a little. Take advantage of him, let him treat you. He may be masked, but at least there's something under the mask.

MELCHIOR. Do you believe in God?

THE MASKED MAN. Depends on the circumstances.

MELCHIOR. Will you tell me who invented gunpowder?

THE MASKED MAN. Berthold Schwarz — alias Konstantin Anklitzen — a Franciscan monk at Freiburg im Breisgau around the year 1330.

MORITZ. I wish he'd lost the recipe!

THE MASKED MAN. You'd only have hanged yourself!

MELCHIOR. What do you think about morals?

THE MASKED MAN. Hey, kid — am I your student?

MELCHIOR. How should I know what you are!

MORITZ. Don't fight! — Please don't fight! What's the point! — What are we sitting here for, two living men and one dead one at two in the morning in the cemetery, if we're going to fight like a bunch of drunks! — I expect it to be a pleasure and a privilege to attend these proceedings. — If you're going to fight, I'll put my head under my arm and go away.

MELCHIOR. You're the same old hand-wringer!

THE MASKED MAN. The ghost has a point. One shouldn't forget one's dignity. — Morals I understand to be the real product of two imaginary quantities. The imaginary quantities are Supposed To and Want To. The product is called Morals and its reality cannot be denied.

MORITZ. I wish you'd told me that before! — My morals were the death of me. It was because of my parents that I picked up a gun. "Honor thy father and mother that thy days shall be long." The scripture looked phenomenally silly in my case.

THE MASKED MAN. Don't delude yourself, my friend. Your mother and father would have died of that as little as you. In strict point of fact, they would have done their raging and storming simply for the good of their health.

MELCHIOR. That may be true as far as it goes. — But I can tell you positively, sir, that if I'd gone ahead and given Moritz my hand just now, it would have been solely and exclusively the fault of my morals.

THE MASKED MAN. That's exactly why you're *not* Moritz!

MORITZ. I really don't think the difference is that essential — at least not so compelling that you couldn't have chanced to meet *me* too, Mr. *Stranger,* when I was trotting through the alders with the gun in my pocket.

THE MASKED MAN. You don't remember me? Even at the last instant you were still standing between *death* and *life,* weren't you? — Incidentally, in my opinion this is really not the place to prolong such a far-reaching discussion.

MORITZ. Certainly, it's getting chilly, gentlemen! — They dressed me up in my Sunday best, but I'm not wearing any shirt or underwear.

MELCHIOR. Farewell, Moritz. I don't know where this person is taking me. But he is a person …

MORITZ. Don't hold it against me that I tried to kill you, Melchior! It was for old time's sake. — I'd spend my whole life in tears and lamentations if I could go out with you one last time now!

THE MASKED MAN. Everyone has his part in the end — *you,* the soothing awareness of having *nothing;* — *you,* the enervating doubts about *everything.* — Farewell.

MELCHIOR. Goodbye, Moritz! I truly appreciate your showing up again. We spent so many cloudless happy days together in fourteen years! I promise you, no matter what happens now, even if my personality changes a dozen times in the coming years, no matter how good or bad things get, I'll never forget you ...

MORITZ. Thank you, thank you, dear one.

MELCHIOR. ... And if I ever get to be an old man with gray hair, maybe you of all people will be closer to me again than everyone I've spent my life with.

MORITZ. Thank you. — Good luck on your journey, gentlemen! — Don't let me keep you any longer.

THE MASKED MAN. Come on, boy! *(The Masked Man links arms with Melchior and moves away over the graves with him.)*

MORITZ. *(Alone.)* — Here I sit with my head on my arm. — The moon covers its face, unveils itself again, and doesn't look the least bit smarter. — — So I'll return to my plot, straighten my cross, which that maniac kicked over so inconsiderately, and when everything's in order I'll lie down on my back again, warm my bones on the decay, and smile ...

End of Play

NOTES

page 17 *baby:* The German word is *kind,* and Mrs. Bergmann can be made more archaic and provincial by substituting "child" for "baby" in every scene in which she appears.

page 19 *Altona:* A major port near Hamburg.

page 21 *Lolo:* Presumably a dog.

page 36 *Faust:* With the aid of Mephistopheles, Faust seduces the virtuous and simple Gretchen and makes her pregnant. She drowns the baby, is imprisoned, refuses Faust's offer of rescue, and is executed for the murder (but she goes to heaven).

page 40 *two and a half years:* A slight inconsistency. Mrs. Bergmann has just said that Ina has been married exactly two years.

page 42 *seven:* Another inconsistency. Hansy has just counted six paintings, and he is about to refer to the murder in progress as his "seventh."

page 43 *Jehoshaphat:* The Valley of Jehoshaphat, where the Last Judgment will be held. (Joel 3:11–15)

page 43 *Heliogabalus:* Emperor of Rome (218–222), notorious for his debaucheries, died at the age of seventeen.

page 43 *Moritura me salutat:* "Those doomed to death salute me."

page 43 *Saint Agnes:* "Agnes was little more than a child; she refused to consider marriage, and consecrated her maidenhood to God; when persecution broke out she left home and offered herself for martyrdom; she resisted all threats, and was executed by being stabbed in the throat." (Donald Attwater, *The Penguin Dictionary of Saints*)

page 48 *It isn't fair of you to make me dizzy: Ihr solltet kein tolles Spiel mit dem Schwindel treiben! Schwindel* can mean either "dizziness" or "fraud"/"deception"/"humbug," and an alternate reading of this line might be "You shouldn't play these crazy games with the swindle!" The literal translation is funnier and contains a suggestion of the more figurative translation.

page 48 *Priapus Club:* Priapus was the Greco-Roman god of fertility and virility; his rites were orgiastic.

page 51   *cattails:* In the original they're mulleins — wildflowers with clublike flower heads.

page 56   *agglutinative Volapük:* An artificial universal language, a precursor of Esperanto.

page 57   *I Corinthians 12:15:* This reads: "If the foot should say, 'Because I am not a hand, I do not belong to the body,' that would not make it any less a part of the body." The sentiment quoted by Bleekhead is from Romans 8:28.

page 62   *fifteen-year-old daughter:* She is, of course, only fourteen.

page 63   *Moab:* Melchior is thinking of racy Bible stories. Moab was Lot's child by his elder daughter; Lot also impregnated his younger daughter. Tamar dressed as a prostitute to lure her father-in-law, Judah, into sex. Nashti, the daughter of the Babylonian King Belshazzar, was beheaded by her husband for refusing to strip naked at a banquet on the Sabbath. Abishag was a beautiful concubine of King David.

page 65   *Blaud's Pills:* For the treatment of anemia; named after the French physician P. Blaud.

page 66   *dropsy:* The old term for edema, the swelling of soft tissues.

page 76   *So I'll return to my plot … :* Moritz's last sentence is in the present tense, which in German can convey either an action that is imminent (as I've translated it) or one that is presently occurring: "So I return to my plot … "